Leaders of Global Impact

Lori A. McNeil, Tim Storey, Eric Ranks
Carolyn Rubin, Joni B. Redick-Yundt
Azadeh Yaraghi, Alka Sharma, Crystal L. Privett,
Jose Escobar, Melody Woods, Maryann Castello

Legal Disclaimer

LEADERS OF GLOBAL IMPACT Copyright © 2024 MPOWERED WORD PUBLISHING. All rights reserved worldwide. No part of this material may be used, reproduced, distributed or transmitted in any form and by any means whatsoever, including without limitation photocopying, recording or other electronic or mechanical methods or by any information storage and retrieval system, without the prior written permission from the author, except for brief excerpts in a review. This book is intended to provide general information only. Neither the author nor publisher provides any legal or other professional advice. If you need professional advice, you should seek advice from the appropriate licensed professional. This book does not provide complete information on the subject matter covered. This book is not intended to address specific requirements, either for an individual or an organization. This book is intended to be used only as a general guide, and not as a sole source of information on the subject matter. While the author has undertaken diligent efforts to ensure accuracy, there is no guarantee of accuracy or of no errors, omissions, or typographical errors. Any slights of people or organizations are unintentional. The author and publisher shall have no liability or responsibility to any person or entity and hereby disclaim all liability, including without limitation, liability for consequential damages regarding any claim, loss or damage that may be incurred, or alleged to have been incurred, directly or indirectly, arising out of the information provided in this book.

Connect with MPowered Word Publishing
www.spiritualtouch11@gmail.com

Copyright © 2024 by MPOWERED PUBLISHING

All rights reserved. No part of this publication may be reproduced or transmitted in any form or by any means, electronic, or mechanical, including photocopying, recording, or by any information storage and retrieval system.

~ Table of Contents ~

Content

Foreword 7

Tim Storey

Introduction 9

Lori A. McNeil

Chapter 1: Dream Bigger, Live Better: A Journey of Purpose, Impact and Legacy 12

Erik Ranks

Chapter 2: Quite Simply Me............. 23

Alka Sharma

Chapter 3: Life Legacy: It's all about the Journey Not the Destination............26

Maryann Castello

Chapter 4: Reveal your one Idea: The Foundation of Your Unique Brand.... 35

Azadeh Yaraghi

Chapter 5: Making Every Moment Matter............................... 48

Melody Woods

Chapter 6: Illuminating Healthcare: An Enduring Legacy...................58

Carolyn Rubin

Chapter 7: The Million Dollar Journey: Cultivating Resilience, Empowering Dreams, Creating Legacy....... 69

Joni B. Redick-Yundt

Chapter 8: A Legacy of Hope...79

Crystal. L. Privett

Chapter 9: Leadership, Excellence, & Legacy............................. 90

Jose Escobar

~ Foreword ~
TIM STOREY

"There's a difference between wanting to be a leader who creates impact and actually having a guide like Leaders of Global Impact to show you how to make it happen."

Occasionally, I come across someone who makes me stop, look, listen, and pay attention. In traveling to over seventy-five countries of the world you get to meet a wide range of people, some of whom create a lasting impression. When I first met Lori McNeil, I intuitively knew she was someone to pay attention to. She is top level. Her ability to help other people see and do is far beyond how many other leadership experts show up. She builds. She builds up organizations. She builds up people. She opens opportunities.

That is exactly what she does here. In this new book she pulls the curtain back on creating more than just demonstrating success in business, she models a way and offers the opportunity for others to have their 'spotlight moment.'

When I say that her understanding of leadership is top level, I want you to know what I mean, you don't find many coaching programs that are created by someone with a 20-year career in education like Lori. She used her skillset to launch her signature coaching program – teaching others how to BUILD their legacy. She doesn't just say she's going to show you what to do, she systematically gives you step-by-step instruction with tools to implement, because she has done it herself.

Great legacies are few and far between and this book goes moves past merely talking about legacy, it exemplifies how you can change lives through building legacy.

The past decade has shown me that there is no shortage of people who study great leaders, but I am noticing that not everyone who studies leaders become great leaders. It is a unique gift to combine knowledge with specific and measurable action steps that genuinely move the needle in your life. Lori McNeil has seen first-hand the legacies of some of the most successful entrepreneurs and knows what it takes to start, lead and build a legacy that lasts. She also has seen what causes t I hem to fail.

Getting an insider's view on how Lori helps others create their legacies is a great opportunity for you. She demonstrates that here by taking the sidelight while showcasing what others are building. It's time to start leading your life so you can create your legacy. Read the stories from those who are doing it…. Making the impact. Creating the influence. Building their legacy.

Thank you for creating a platform for legacy builders to be seen, to be heard, and to build upon. When people are willing to share how they have helped others, you better pay attention. Pay attention to Leaders of Global Impact. I Love how Lori puts it; "You can't buy a Legacy, you build one."

~INTRODUCTION~

Lori A. McNeil

Many entrepreneurs launch businesses to have more control over their time and money while doing something meaningful. This was true for me. Nearing the completion of a successful twenty-five-year career in education, I pondered the next chapter of my life and what impact I could have with the experiences and tools acquired over the years.

My desire was to travel and impact those outside of the traditional classroom setting. As I grew into the entrepreneurial lifestyle, teaching, and coaching entrepreneurs the foundational tools needed for success, I noticed a crucial, necessary tools missing – a clear vision for Legacy. This went beyond, "why do you do what you do?"

Recognizably, an important question to answer, however building a true Legacy is something that impacts lives more profoundly than most realize. The deeper I dug into understanding Legacy; I discovered common threads which lead to specific steps crucial in creating legacy.

Building that Legacy does not magically occur when you retire, when your kids go off to college, move out, or when you have enough zeros in your bank account. Contrary to what many influencers believe, it has nothing to do with your name on a building. Building a Legacy takes focused, intentional daily actions. True Legacy will outlive you.

Throughout my career, I have discovered and sharpened right- steps which produce a focused attention towards building a Legacy that positions one to create an impact grander than you ever thought possible.

Legacy Builders is a unique process which unfolds those steps necessary in creating that true Legacy. Once entrepreneurs realize there is more to building a business than an overflowing bank account, they begin to think much more about the impact their business has, and truly begin to grow richer. When we realize that our businesses hold impact power (as a tool), our mindset shifts to producing vastly different actions as we now operate with a deeper purpose in each moment.

Allowing ourselves to think bigger, to have faith over fear, now opens a whole new world of possibilities. It can be scary yet rewarding. Most entrepreneurs truly desire to help people. It is sad that many spend years working hard to create a business not designed for maximum impact, so much untapped potential. But why? For some, maybe they just really do not know that something is missing. For others, they don't know what they don't know. For many, its fear holding them back… or laziness. Laziness to honestly dig into those foundational tools necessary to build something amazing. It's truly remarkable how fear and laziness can kill genuine growth and potential.

Only YOU know the truth about what is happening. Only YOU can tell your story. Only YOU can build YOUR Legacy. Nobody can be you. YOU are uniquely qualified to do what you do. You have everything you need to amazingly impact the world. I often say, "Your internal tools make you uniquely qualified to solve external problems."

The global leaders in this book have all achieved much success and learned many lessons that have gotten them to the point in their lives where they are serving people with greater purpose and impact. A true leader's work is never done, and each of them continue to push themselves out their comfort zone in order to become the best version of themselves that the world needs. Their stories are inspirational and life changing if you allow for them to be. **You can't buy a legacy, you BUILD it.**

~ Chapter 1 ~
Dream Bigger, Live Better: A Journey of Purpose, Impact, and Legacy

Erik Ranks

Life rarely unfolds like that of a perfectly scripted story. More often, its an unpredictable journey punctuated by exhilarating highs and gut-wrenching lows. My own path has been a crucible of both. From the sudden loss of my father in 2019, a soul-crushing event, to battles with health, as well as personal failures. All these trials along with a myriad of triumphs have shaped my understanding of purpose and the desire to leave a lasting positive impact. This chapter is more than just a recount of my life, its a testament to the power of resilience and the human spirits capacity to transform adversity into a force for good.

Childhood Challenges and Unwavering Faith My understanding of pain, both physical and mental, began early in life. Diagnosed with Leukemia at age five, I was confronted with a battle that seemed insurmountable for someone of such a young age. During this time, my father served in the Air Force, and we were stationed at Loring AFB in Limestone, Maine. My illness escalated to such a degree that I required an emergency transfer, known as an Air-Evac, to Bethesda Naval Hospital in Bethesda, Maryland (currently Walter Reed National Military Medical Center) for advanced testing and treatment.

It was during this life-altering experience at Bethesda Naval Hospital that I discovered my own uniqueness. A remarkable physical trait was revealed: I have a horseshoe-shaped kidney, a distinctive feature that I came to recognize as a symbol of my individuality and resilience. This unique aspect of my anatomy taught me to embrace and value the things that set me apart.

Amidst these trials, the support of my family, combined with the fervent prayers and blessings from our church community, enveloped me in a cocoon of hope and strength. This collective support was instrumental in my recovery and played a pivotal role in shaping my early understanding of faith, God, and the power of community. My miraculous improvement in health not only marked a physical triumph but also instilled in me a profound belief in divine intervention, a belief that would become a guiding force through future challenges.

My adolescent years, fraught with the challenges of bullying and dyslexia, were instrumental in teaching me the importance of perseverance. These experiences taught me that with determination and the right support, one can overcome even the most daunting obstacles. My father's steadfast advocacy in my struggle with dyslexia not only helped me navigate through these challenges but also instilled in me the invaluable power of advocacy itself. His dedication to finding tools and innovative strategies for me to comprehend and communicate was transformative.

This phase of my life was pivotal in learning to adapt to various situations and in understanding the significance of a strong support network – lessons that have continually echoed throughout my life. These formative experiences, combined with a serious health battle and the discovery of my unique physical trait, laid a robust foundation for my resilience, and deepened my faith. They highlighted the crucial roles of family, community, and prayer in overcoming adversity, teaching me that our distinct traits and challenges shape us into resilient, faith-driven individuals. To those facing their own battles, remember: your unique challenges are not just hurdles but are defining elements of your character.

Embrace your individuality, draw strength from your unique journey, and see your trials as opportunities to grow and inspire others. Facing and Overcoming Adversity As a young man who had overcome Leukemia, I carried a sense of invincibility, believing that I could withstand any challenge life threw at me. However, this belief was dramatically tested when, at eighteen.

I was involved in a near-fatal car accident. The accident was a harsh awakening to the fragility of life leaving me profoundly shaken, bruised, and with a broken femur. This event marked the beginning of a series of hardships that would further challenge my perception of invincibility.

In my early twenties, I went through a painful divorce which plunged me into a deep depression. This difficult period of my life culminated in an accidental overdose on antidepressants, a critical point that highlights the importance of self-care and mental health. These experiences were filled with pain and despair, yet they served as crucial turning points. They taught me valuable lessons about the critical importance of seeking help during difficult times.

During the summer of 2014, my life was once again turned upside down by an unexpected health crisis. What I thought was mild fatigue quickly escalated into a dire, life-threatening medical situation. I found myself engaged in a fierce battle against severe internal bleeding, caused by an undiagnosed autoimmune disease. This condition led to a critical state of anemia, bringing me alarmingly close to the brink of death.

This harrowing ordeal required multiple blood transfusions and an intense, three-week period of enduring multiple daily endoscopies and colonoscopies across two hospitals to try and control the bleeding. A particularly critical moment occurred during an emergency procedure in the ICU when I aspirated while under anesthesia, causing my stomach to herniate through my diaphragm. This incident, which could have been fatal if it had occurred outside the ICU, underscored the fragility and unpredictability of my condition. With this newly diagnosed autoimmune disease, doctors warned me that it would more than likely happen again.

Not wanting to go through that experience again, I began researching preventative measures. Being diagnosed with Type II diabetes and Non-Alcoholic Steatohepatitis (NASH) at the time, I was intrigued to learn the crucial role nutrition plays in our overall wellness. It was during this research that I discovered the Ketogenic diet and how m diseases and illnesses were linked to metabolic syndrome.

With everything I learned, a sense of purpose ignited within me to not only improve my own life but also to positively impact the lives of others. This lifestyle played a significant role in my next four years. I witnessed the impacts of proper nutrition on my personal life and others that I helped, my internal bleeding stayed at bay, and I lost over 100 lbs.

The year 2019 marked a period of profound personal losses and challenges that deeply impacted my life. Among these, the most heart-wrenching was the sudden loss of my father. I vividly remember the day, Sunday, August 18th, 2019, when he called me, extending an invitation to join him and my mother for dinner at their house, about 45 minutes away.

For reasons I can no longer recall, I declined his invitation and asked to come over the next weekend instead. This decision has since become a source of deep regret. Tragically, that very night, he unexpectedly passed away in his sleep. This missed opportunity to spend those final precious hours with him plunged me into a state of grief and emotional turmoil and has left an indelible mark on my heart.

Losing my father unexpectedly created a profound void in my life and taught me the value of time spent with loved ones. It emphasized the importance of being present in our relationships and the deep emotional connections we share with family. This served as a stark reminder of life's transient nature and underscored the importance of being truly present with those we hold dear. This experience has reinforced the necessity to treasure and prioritize these vital relationships in our everyday lives.

Just two months after the loss of my father, I encountered yet another formidable health challenge: a ruptured esophagus caused by the hernia created years before that necessitated immediate, high-risk surgery. This procedure was fraught with danger, carrying a daunting survival rate of less than 50%. The gravity of the situation and the slim odds of survival once again brought me face-to-face with the fragility and preciousness of life.

Remarkably, I survived the surgery, a feat that even my surgeon attributed to some form of divine intervention. He expressed that my survival was not solely the result of medical expertise but a higher power guiding him, acknowledging that he had not encountered such a case more than once or twice in his 18-year career. This acknowledgment of a higher power at work during the surgery resonated deeply with me. I felt an intense sense of spiritual presence in the operating room, believing not only in a Higher Power's influence but also in the comforting presence of my father. After being released from the hospital, I faced a significant adjustment in my daily life: I was put on a feeding tube, with 90% of my calories coming from this source. This change was both physically and mentally challenging as I had been adhering to a strict ketogenic diet for years, but now found myself limited to a liquid diet high in sugars via the feeding tube for several months which led to unexpected weight gain.

The COVID pandemic in 2020 added another layer of complexity and stress to my situation.

Navigating the restrictions and uncertainties of the pandemic while adjusting to a new way of feeding myself tested my resilience and adaptability. It was a time that demanded a re-evaluation of my approach to health and nutrition and required me to develop new strategies to maintain my well-being in the face of these unexpected life changes.

Confronting an undiagnosed autoimmune disease and critical medical procedures, including a near-death experience, I unearthed a resilience within me that defies odds. These trials transcended mere survival, embodying lessons in resilience, faith, and the marvels of medicine. They taught me to cherish every moment, live with purpose, and value the support of loved ones. My journey is a testament to the human spirits indomitable strength and the transformative power of perseverance. It is a compelling reminder that our darkest times can forge our strongest selves and that, in adversity, we can find life's truest gifts. Building a Legacy through Service

In 2012, my path to impactful service and meaningful change crystallized with the founding of The Veterans Connection (TVC), a 501(c)(3) nonprofit dedicated to championing the cause of Veterans. Initially focused on guiding Veterans through the complex process to secure their rightful benefits, the sight of their struggles against bureaucratic barriers was both heartrending and a call to action. Through TVC, we embarked on a journey to not only assist but to uplift and empower, ensuring that our heroes receive the recognition and support they so richly deserve.

As I observed the growing mental health crisis and alarming rise in suicide rates among Veterans and first responders during the Covid-19 pandemic, the mission of TVC evolved significantly. This shift redirected our focus towards providing vital mental health resources, aimed at preventing this tragic loss of life. Motivated by a deep commitment to this cause, I actively sought out conversations with industry thought leaders, healthcare professionals, and the Veteran community.

Through these vital exchanges, we aimed to elevate awareness and inspire meaningful change, addressing the urgent need for mental health resources and support for those who have bravely served.

The Veterans Connection now employs a four-phase approach to enhance the quality of life for Veterans: Connect, Empower, Align, and Thrive. Each phase is designed to address specific needs, from fostering a sense of community and belonging to providing access to alternative healing solutions and career development programs.

2022 marked a significant expansion of my dedication to supporting our heroes with the launch of 22 Salute Spirits & Coffee, made possible through the collaboration of friends and fellow Veteran-dependents. This venture goes beyond typical business objectives, symbolizing a heartfelt mission to promote mental health awareness and aid for Veterans and first responders. We proudly allocate a portion of our proceeds to The Veterans Connection (TVC) and other Veteran support initiatives, ensuring that every purchase directly aids in providing essential resources and backing for those who have honorably served our nation.

When I founded 22 Salute, I never anticipated the profound emotional resonance our brand would evoke when sampling our products. In numerous instances, customers would pause at our demo booth and learn about our mission. The depth of their reactions has been both unexpected and deeply moving.

Many, often with tears in their eyes shared their stories with us, sharing heartfelt thanks for our commitment to mental health and recounting individual experiences of how suicide has touched their lives. These moments of raw emotional connection, unfolding unexpectedly in grocery store aisles, have been a powerful testament to the impact of our work. They serve as a poignant reminder that our legacy extends far beyond a business venture—it reaches into the hearts and lives of individual's, resonating in ways I never imagined.

Moving forward, my commitment to supporting Veterans and first responders through The Veterans Connection and 22 Salute Spirits & amp; Coffee is stronger than ever. These initiatives reflect my dedication to serving others and my passion for making a difference. By aligning my personal passions with these meaningful causes, I aim to contribute to mental health awareness, suicide prevention, and the promotion of overall well-being. These ventures stand as a testament to the power of social entrepreneurship in creating positive change and supporting those who have sacrificed so much for our country.

Personal Struggles as Catalysts for Change

Reflecting on my journey, I realize the importance of leaving a legacy that resonates beyond my time. Surviving multiple near-death experiences has instilled in me a sense of urgency to make a positive impact, not just as an individual but as part of a larger narrative of service and compassion. I want to guide others to find their purpose and passions, and the realization that with compassion and community no darkness is insurmountable. Our time here is fleeting, but the legacy we leave behind endures. I am dedicating my years to serving those who served us, helping heal wounds both physical and psychological.

My personal motto, and quote; Dream Bigger, Live Better; is more than just words; it is a philosophy that guides my actions. It embodies the belief in pursuing lofty aspirations while enhancing the lives of those around us. This mantra has been the cornerstone of my efforts, whether through volunteering, advocacy, or social entrepreneurship. Dreaming bigger, reaching out a hand, speaking words of encouragement, offering comfort food, raising funds to train service dogs or simply sitting with someone in their darkest hour – these small acts can have ripples of impact reaching farther than I will ever know.

Embarking on a journey to build a legacy does not necessarily require grand gestures; it can start with simple acts rooted in our passions and aligning them with a purpose that transcends mere personal satisfaction. Whether it is spreading warmth through cooking for the homeless or uplifting spirits with music in nursing homes, every small step contributes to a greater good. It is about turning what we love into a force for positive change in the world around us.

When applying our passions towards noble causes, we not only innovate but also address critical needs in society, such as supporting our veterans and First Responders. Our unique talents become vehicles for impactful change, allowing us to honor the sacrifices of these heroes and contribute to their well-being. Through initiatives like The Veterans Connection and 22 Salute Spirits and Coffee, I have experienced firsthand the profound impact of aligning passion with purpose. When we find that intersection of passion and purpose, we not only enrich our own lives but also forge a legacy that makes a meaningful difference in the lives of others.

As I continue move forward on this path, I invite you to join me in this mission of positivity and purpose, discovering your passions and see how they can serve a greater cause. My journey teaches us that resilience is a universal trait we can all foster. Whether you are facing health challenges, emotional turmoil, or personal losses, know that each step, no matter how small, is a stride towards resilience and making a difference in not just your life, but also in others. Remember, your struggles are not just obstacles; they are opportunities to discover your Why and contribute to a legacy that extends beyond our own lives.

In the journey of building a long-lasting legacy, the obstacles we encounter often serve as our greatest teachers. What challenges have shaped your journey? How can you use these experiences to create a positive impact in your community? I challenge you to take one step this week towards turning QQ2your struggles into a force for good. Your story, your passion, and your willingness to engage are vital pieces in this mosaic of change.

Eric Ranks

https://www.ericranks.com/

~ Chapter 2 ~
ALKA SHARMA
QUITE SIMPLY ME….

In contemplating the future, I have discovered a profound truth: the act of looking up, looking forward, and relentlessly pursuing our goals is not just insightful, but transformative. This philosophy is deeply rooted in my belief in the power of legacy – the desire to leave an indelible mark on the world, to begin "Looking Past my Future," and, particularly for women, empowering them to forge paths of strength and success.

My journey has not been without its trials. I have navigated through dark times and faced traumatic moments within my marriage. Feeling isolated and ostracized from my family, I encountered profound loneliness.

Yet, it was in these moments of despair that I found my greatest strength. Stepping out from the shadows of adversity, I turned my gaze upwards, drawing strength and courage from a higher power, which for me is God. This newfound resilience enabled me to look forward with determination, charting a course towards a life marked by success and fulfillment.

Today, my life is a testament to this transformation – a journey from victimhood to victory. Every decade, I find myself chasing a new version of my 'hero' – the future self that embodies my aspirations and dreams. The proudest moments of my life are not just personal achievements, but the realization that the life I have built and the ideas I've promoted are creating a ripple effect. This impact empowers women everywhere to recognize and embrace their self-worth and dignity, even after overcoming their own hardships, and to see the grace they possess within

My mission is clear: to leave behind a legacy built on the pillars of strength, determination, and courage. It fills me with immense pride to know that my efforts to empower women continue to shine brightly, illuminating paths for others to follow. I eagerly anticipate the future, hopeful that my work will persist, offering a beacon of hope amidst the despair and struggles we may face. I envision a world where women can boldly declare, "I am the embodiment of strength and courage, leading the way towards empowerment."

As an advocate for women's empowerment, my commitment is to make a difference, touching lives one woman at a time. In this unity, there is immense strength; together, we are an unstoppable force. United in our purpose, we stand as a testament to the power of collective resilience and empowerment.

~ ALKA SHARMA ~

Alka, Sharma is a Real Estate Investor residing in Toronto, Ontario, Canada. Alka guides her clients seeking investment strategies carve out their niche to success. Alka takes her time to make sure her client's needs are met is her utmost concern. Alka lives life to the fullest, her passions when she is not working are rock climbing, she got into three years ago loves to constantly challenge herself. She is highly competitive in nature. She is an accomplished professional ballroom dancer competed since 2004, recognised for her talents, achieved recognition amongst her peers and judges. Alka is extremely grateful for all of her experiences that have shaped her today as a successful entrepreneur, real estate investor.

~ Chapter 3 ~

MARYANN CASTELLO

LIFE LEGACY: IT'S ALL ABOUT THE JOURNEY NOT THE DESTINATION

What is legacy? Legacy can be defined in many ways. Some may define it as what you are leaving to your family, whether it be money, property, personal items, etc. I define it as what is the impact you leave for the world when you leave this earth. Here's "my story" …

I was born and raised in New Jersey. I am not a fan of the winter months. I never was from childhood to adulthood. But I stayed in New Jersey. Why? Because of something called family. We are close-knit. I am the youngest of three children. Even though I was the youngest, I was not spoiled. My parents raised each of us teaching us love, respect, kindness, goals, faith, and life lessons. During our childhood, our mom experienced a lot of health challenges.

As a young child, I did grasp the understanding of how serious they were. My dad would work several jobs to provide for all of us. My mom would work part-time when she could, and she ran the house like a tight ship. Even with all my mom's health challenges, she had a wicked sense of humor. By wicked, I mean she was hilarious. She faced adversity with laughter. I must admit, I believe growing up seeing things that I did, helped make me the woman I am today. Let me explain.

We would help around the house. They were called chores. Each of us had some. We did not collect an allowance for them. We were taught they are a labor of love. We washed dishes, folded clean laundry, or vacuumed, etc. I may have not realized it at the time, but everything we did around the house taught us life skills. In a word, responsibilities. Sometimes, my parents would have us stay with our grandparents for a duration if my mom needed to be hospitalized. Thank God, my parents taught us responsibilities. I remember my paternal grandmother in her loving way requested my brother and I do chores. During those times, I realized how much I missed my mom and what she must have been going through. I may have only been at my grandmother's a couple of weeks, but it felt like months. When we would return home, my parents never missed a beat, my dad working and my mom making sure were all doing what we were supposed to be doing.

I was a great student in school over the years. I had 4.0 averages, honor roll, awards, and scholarships. My grades amazed me because my sister was also a 4.0 student, but she really put in a lot of work by giving teachers more than they asked for. Me, well, I think I did enough to get by. Yes, I understood everything I was doing. I was wise beyond my years, so I was bored a lot in school. I felt like I could be doing more. In senior year in high school, I was on the work program where you would go to school for half day and then go to your job and work your scheduled hours. I was a very hard worker. I worked many hours with two part-time jobs. So much so, I earned awards and a partial scholarship.

All my experiences prepared me for the work force. I worked in corporate jobs for over two and a half decades. My last corporate "job" lasted for seventeen years. I put my blood, sweat and tears into that job. I worked my way up the corporate ladder into management positions. I became the "go-to" person for many of the big responsibilities. I liked what I did but thought to myself, there must be more to life. I continued to do it day-after-day, week-after-week, month-after-month, year-after-year. It's all I knew, but I knew deep down inside I was not truly happy. Then it happened.

My life scare. It was the year 2000. I was not feeling myself, dizziness, extreme fatigue, heart palpitations, temperature change fluctuations, panic attacks, undesired body changes and more. I was diagnosed with hyperthyroid and prescribed medication which I developed a severe allergic reaction and found myself in a hospital, had surgery, and became allergic to most allopathic medications. By what I can only describe by divine intervention, I was led to holistic modalities which changed my life. I healed completely. I felt better than I ever did!

At this point everything changed for me. My entire being changed. I realized the unhappiness I felt for all those years led to a physical manifestation in my body and now I had complete control of my body. When did I get this realization? I noticed on good days; I felt like I could conquer anything. On not so good days, I felt physically and mentally drained. That is, it!! I was experiencing the true feeling of empowerment. By being in constant awareness on every level of my being; physical, emotional, mental, and spiritual, I was able to achieve complete homeostasis utilizing various holistic modalities. I was fascinated. I researched day and night with the philosophies and teachings from Louise Hay, Dr. Wayne Dyer, and so many more. It validated my experiences, and I got to work.

I started to write a daily journal of what I wanted or wished for. I wrote down the good things and bad things that happened daily. It was shocking to me that the more I journaled the more negative my entries were getting. I felt like I wanted to give up, but I did not. I kept working at it. I remember going to sleep completely exhausted one night and I had a dream. Yes, I had a dream. That dream changed my perspective because it was everything I ever wanted in life. It made me work harder. I continued my journal with more positive entries, meditated, recited affirmations, and even made a vision board so I could "feel" what I wanted. I did this every day. After a couple of weeks, things changed for the better. When I saw things changing and felt that I **DID** have the power to change my thoughts, I knew I could change my life. During the day, I went to work. In the evenings, I went to school. I was feeling empowered because I was being true to myself for the first time in my life.

I redefined my life. New healthy lifestyle, new goals, more research, etc. I opened my own business. Yes, my *own* business. It was *mine*. Neos Zoe LLC, "New Life Through Balanced Living." It was small and I did continue working my full-time corporate job, but I saw clients in the evenings. By continuing with all my journaling, meditating, reciting affirmations, studying my vision board, I added prayer. Never underestimate the power of prayer. The more I studied faith the more powerful I became. I knew I was never alone. You see, I never realized why certain things happened to me up to this point. I did not mention to you that from a young child to a grown adult, I loved to sing. I sang every minute I could. Even working a corporate job, I had my own side business working several nights a week being a disc jockey, hosting karaoke at various venues and providing live lead vocals for celebrations. When I had my health scare, after the surgery, doctors explained to me that I would not be able to sing again. I was devastated for years. When I discovered the power of prayer, this all changed

At this point, there was a big life change again. I was no longer employed at my corporate job. At first it was scary yet exhilarating. I had my own business, now I was forced to make it full-time. This is where I am going to explain another divine intervention. I was helping a client, Donna, who had cerebral palsy and was not able to walk. She allowed me to do applied kinesiology on her and her body actually showed what it was lacking. She followed all the recommendations we spoke about, and she was healing.

She was walking using canes instead of a wheelchair. Not only was she a client, but she also became my dearest friend. She believed in me. She gave me a referral of a lifetime. She introduced me to Grammy Award Winner, Producer and Arranger, Tony Camillo. He came to me for a healing session, but then the ultimate happened. After a session, he said to me that "a little birdie told me that you sing." I knew that "little birdie" was Donna. I was shy about it because I did not sing for years and right before me, stood "Thee Tony Camillo!" He asked me to sing. That is when the deep sweat from nerves started for me, but he listened to every word intently. When I finished, I was actually shaking, and he looked me directly in my eyes and with his warm smile said, "Let's work together." Pinch me!! From there, he introduced me to Dr. Otto Jorgensen. He was terrific. He believed in healthy lifestyle approaches, and we combined our talents. He then referred someone. Singer, songwriter, guitarist, producer, and arranger, Ryche Chlanda. After several healing sessions with Ryche, we built a genuine friendship. Before I knew it, Tony wrote lyrics for a song for me and asked Ryche to write the music, and we worked and recorded it at Dr. Otto Jorgensen's house, all with Donna by my side through all of it!

I will recap here what all happened from learning the power of empowerment. I became a Board-Certified Holistic Health Practitioner and a NJ Licensed Massage Therapist specializing in clinical nutrition and medical massage, a Reiki Master Teacher and Practitioner and an Ordained Minister Practitioner. I have taught classes at the Academy of Natural Health Sciences and served on advisory boards for public schools Departments of Special Services. What could potentially happen from here? Yes, there is more!!

While working at my new office in my own business, I received a call that would change my life again. A company reached out to me to discuss potentially co-authoring a book. I thought it was a telemarketing call. Do you know the ones you receive when you start a new business? But something in my "gut" told me "Maryann, just shut up and listen!" So, I did. With my new fan club, Donna, Tony, Dr. Jorgensen, and Ryche, they told me "Go for it!" Guess what happened? I got selected to be one of thirty-six authors worldwide to co-author a book with Jack Canfield, the co-author of the "Chicken Soup for the Soul" Series. Not just any book. A Best-Seller! "The Road to Success, Volume 2." It was on the Top 20 Books as seen on Amazon.com's Direct Marketing Best Sellers List. I won an Editor's Choice Award for my outstanding contribution to the book. I was invited to a Red-Carpet Event in Hollywood, CA and was the recipient of a 2016 Quilly® Award and became a member of the National Academy of Best-Selling Authors™.

Wait, it does not end there. Would you believe I was offered radio and television opportunities? Yes, it is true. I was featured on Spotlight Television, "Neos Zoe – New Life with Maryann Castello" along with Co-Host, Frank MacKay and currently host my own radio shows, "Bare All," "Health & Wellness," and "Liberty Bell Smack" on WWDB-AM TALK 860 in Philadelphia, PA, as an expert in various holistic modalities and currently host my own TV Show, with "Bare♥All "with Maryann Castello." It is a New Interview, Lifestyle and Healthy Living Television Show…Where I Get to the Heart of The Matter and can be found weekly on DBTV on Roku TV, Amazon Fire, and all Smart TV's. I received my second invitation to a Red-Carpet Event in Hollywood, CA and was the recipient of an EXPY® Award for Media & Communication from the National Association of Experts, Writers, and Speakers™. I was then selected as one of America's Premier Experts™ and I was quoted in Talk Nation Magazine with Frank MacKay and NJ Discover with Calvin Schwartz on creating healthy lifestyles. I was even named the VIP Woman of the Year 2015-2016 from the National Association of Professional Woman.

And just when I thought it could not get any better. It did. Ryche and our dear friend, Jay Petsko, a graphic artist, web designer, producer, and filmmaker, listened to me when I said I want to be able to help people and worked with me creating a Meditation DVD and CD "Extreme Chakra Cleansing for A Super-Charged Life" where people can learn how to meditate with their eyes open. Now of all things, I am on stage with Ryche. I am the background vocalist for NEKTAR: The Legendary Rock Band and touring with the band for their 50th Anniversary World Tour. We are currently in the studio recording a new album. That is the power of prayer and empowerment!

It has always been my desire and mission to help each individual person to achieve complete homeostasis by educating them through my teachings of various holistic practices to empower themselves through their healing journey on the physical, emotional, mental, and spiritual levels. I am committed to my own personal growth and continuing education keeping me on the frontier of innovative holistic solutions for achieving optimal health, harmonious living, and lifestyle choices. What is your desire? Do you have a mission?

Legacy. You have read my story that has become my legacy to date. When I sit back and reflect, I recognize how fortunate I am. It has been an exceptionally long process, but my healing journey helped me regain my health and vitality by equipping me to see life experiences from different perspectives. It has not been an easy road. I made many sacrifices to fulfill my life's purpose. There have been many rewards too along the way. I have met so many wonderful people that let me make the mistakes I needed to make, but also helped me elevate above them. I have learned to always believe in yourself. No matter what. It all starts there. Do not let life pass you by. Embrace it.

You are made for greatness. All of us have our own unique gifts to share with others. Love is one of the greatest gifts. For others and yourself, self-. When you can love yourself and empower yourself, life will fall into place. Will there be ups and downs? Sure. There is no such thing as failure. Failure teaches you life lessons. You grow from failure. We learn from failure. Do not ever let it stop you. How will you manage adversity? If you manage it with love and look for solutions, adversity is temporary. All of us have our own successes and challenges. Enjoy every success and work through any challenges. There are so many more experiences to have. We should live every single day to the fullest as we do not know when or how we may leave this world.

Life – it's all about the journey not the destination.

~MARYANN CASTELLO ~

LMT, HHP

TV and Radio Personality/Best-Selling Author/Motivational Speaker Maryann Castello is a Board-Certified Holistic Health Practitioner, NJ Licensed Massage Therapist and CEO/Founder of Neos Zoe LLC, specializing in clinical nutrition, medical massage, reiki master teacher/practitioner, and an ordained minister practitioner. She's taught clinical aromatherapy/detoxification classes and served on public schools Departments of Special Services advisory boards. She is a Best-Selling Author and a TV/Radio personality hosting radio shows and her ownTV show "Bare♥All with Maryann Castello. She's won several awards: 2016 Quilly® Award, Member of National Academy of Best-Selling Authors™, EXPY® Award for Media & Communication from the National Association of Experts, Writers, and Speakers™, Editor's Choice Award, selected as one of America's Premier Experts™ and named the VIP Woman of the Year 2015-2016 from the National Association of Professional Woman. Maryann has a Meditation CD/DVD; Extreme Chakra Cleansing for A Super Charged Life" and is a background vocalist currently touring with NEKTAR: The Legendary Rock Band.

You can connect with Maryann at:

www.facebook.com/Maryann.Castello

Maryann@NeosZoe.com

www.facebook.com/NeosZoellc

~ Chapter 4 ~
Azadeh Yaraghi

REVEAL YOUR ONE IDEA: THE FOUNDATION OF YOUR UNIQUE BRAND

In today's competitive business landscape, differentiation is key, but it's not just about what you sell—it's about championing a unique brand idea. This core concept, your ONE IDEA, is crucial for distinguishing your brand and connecting authentically with your target audience. Not only that, but it is also about discovering and directing your legacy. A legacy that is uniquely you. Understanding the ONE IDEA!

Your ONE IDEA transcends your products or services; it is an embodiment of your core values, beliefs, and what sets you apart. It is not the tangible offerings but the intangible. promises your brand holds that engages your ideal clients at a deeper level.

This central idea acts as your business's guiding light, influencing all strategies and interactions, ensuring they resonate with your audience's values and expectations. It is about creating a consistent, impactful experience that aligns with your brand's essence.

To unearth your ONE IDEA, we must go into self-reflection. Understand your motivations, unique strengths, and what you stand for. This process reveals the heart of your brand, enabling you to communicate a compelling, resonant message to your audience.

Let us have a look at how three distinguished brands do this:

First, Nike. Nike makes shoes, but they sell the idea of EXCELLENCE. When you think of Nike, what story do they tell in their advertisements? They often show athletes at their top of their game, top achievers, who want to accomplish their absolute best. They also show 'normal' people those determined to reach their next level of success – whatever that is to them.

Nike tells you the story of excellence, perseverance, and empowerment. They do not talk about the way the shoe is fabricated and what materials are used. Because those attributes do not inspire. Nike is one of the best marketers on the planet because they know how to tap into our most intrinsic emotions. Their promise is clear… Just do it… and achieve excellence.

What about Coca-Cola. Yes, they make soft drinks, but they sell the idea of HAPPINESS. When you think of Coca-Cola ads, what do you remember? I often remember beautiful people spending time together in a hot place, cool music playing, people having fun… and it is hot… extremely hot! And then there is the Coke can open… euphorically… all the scenes are involved in that moment when it opens… Ahhhhh… the person drinks it.

It is an experience. It is about togetherness and celebration. What Coke does not talk about is that it's made up of water, sugar, and syrup… because, well, who would buy that? Their brand's promise is that if you have Coke at your next gathering, you are sure to surround yourself with happy, memorable moments.

Finally, let us look at Oprah. Oprah is a talk show host, but she sells the idea of COMPASSION. Oprah is many things to many people, but no matter the shows, the magazines, the products, and all her accolades, at the heart of it all is her heart and compassion. If you are an Oprah fan, you know that she is driven and passionate to help build a more holistic, loving, and enlightened humanity.

That is her ONE IDEA and her promise. It is not the shiny gifts given at her shows (albeit and added perk). She has loyal fans because she consistently promises to help people and the planet, aiming to make the world better. This mission is her legacy. Her followers feel inspired and add some of her positive influence on their lives whenever they engage with her.

Connecting with Others

Your ONE IDEA is not only about self-discovery but also about understanding how others perceive and connect with you. Conduct research, engage with your audience, and listen to their feedback. How do they see your brand? What emotions or associations are tied to it? If you asked them to describe you with three adjectives, what would they say? This feedback helps you refine and articulate your ONE IDEA in a way that resonates deeply with your ideal target audience.

Legacy & Passion

Infusing your ONE IDEA into your brand, does not simply clarify your promise, it cultivates legacy. Your brand becomes synonymous with the values and beliefs you stand for, inspiring others to follow. Through consistent branding efforts, you shape how your brand is remembered and perceived, leaving a positive impact on future generations.

When you align your brand with your ONE IDEA, you tap into that deeper sense of purpose and passion. Your brand becomes more than a venture; it becomes a vehicle for expressing your authenticity. By infusing passion into your branding efforts, you inspire others to join your cause, become part of something greater than themselves, thus bettering the world.

Your ONE IDEA has the power to transcend borders and cultures, resonating with people from all walks of life. Through strategic branding initiatives, you can amplify your message and reach a global audience. With a strong brand identity and narrative, you create a ripple effect which extends far beyond your immediate community, driving positive change on a global scale.

Simplifying Business, Cultivating Stronger Bonds

Once your ONE IDEA is crystal clear, it becomes the cornerstone of your decision-making process. It simplifies your business strategy, guiding you in choosing projects, collaborations, and opportunities which align your core values. In marketing, your ONE IDEA becomes the narrative thread that weaves through all your communication channels, creating a cohesive and compelling brand story. In sales, it streamlines your approach, simplifying communication, and adding to the unique value you bring to the table.

Your ONE IDEA is a magnetic force that attracts like-minded individuals who resonate with your vision and vibe. These are not just customers; they are advocates and ambassadors of your brand. Through embodying your

ONE IDEA, you cultivate deeper, more meaningful connections with your audience. This connection goes beyond transactional relationships, fostering loyalty and turning customers into long-term brand enthusiasts.

Finding Your ONE IDEA

Try this exercise (it is more effective to do this activity with someone). Choose a partner who can ask you questions and write down your responses. Then you can focus solely on the exercise without overthinking your answers. The outcomes become clear in the end.

Partner: At the heart of what you do, what do you think is the highest value you offer to your clients?

You: Answer with ONE word. Go with the first thing that comes to you. Do not overthink it! Go with your gut instincts.

Partner: If your clients have access to _____ (insert your answer) _____, what would they achieve next?

You: Answer with ONE word

Partner: If your clients have access to _____ (insert your answer) _____, what would they achieve next?

You: Answer with ONE word

Partner: If your clients have access to _____ (insert your answer) _____, what would they achieve next?

You: Answer with ONE word

Continue this line of questions, continue peeling the onion, and answer until you say: "If they got ___X___ they would be able to achieve anything!"

Your ONE IDEA is usually in the last three answers.

Now, let us examine two case studies to illustrate how you can identify your ONE IDEA and the power it has in shaping a thoughtful brand.

Case Study 1: Dr. Karen

Dr. Karen is a high-performance psychologist, professional speaker, and

Olympian coach. She first approached me to talk about her website. She has been in a growth phase and needed a compelling website to present her services. Most of all, she wanted to get to the heart of her messaging because this was the hardest part for her... finding her voice and her phrasing in writing. Because she was unsure of her unique message, she stopped working on her website content, which delayed her website's completion and potential new opportunities.

When we started working together, I took her through the Brand Workshop to determine the strategy of her brand. When we got to the ONE IDEA exercise and went through the exact line of questions illustrated for you previously, these are the answers she got:

Azadeh: At the heart of what you do, what do you think is the highest value you offer to your clients?

Dr. Karen: **(in this order)**

Growth

Improvement

Performance

Results

Show up at their best.

Handle high pressure.

Shine in their big moments

Satisfaction

Contentment

Empowered

Resilient

Clarity of who they are at their best.

Focus

Self-awareness

Acceptance

Freedom

 When we got to Freedom, she stopped. She said: "If my clients could get access to freedom, they can achieve anything! Wow!" That is, it! We knew we got it! After identifying her ONE IDEA, she crafted a concise brand story that effectively conveyed her message, not just her services. She did this successfully, and we then developed her tagline, "Freedom to Perform™," followed by the content for her website and the website design itself.

 The best compliment anyone can get from their brand is: "this is SO YOU!" Dr. Karen got just that in addition to a heightened confidence in her known as app developers who handle complex projects delivering high-quality work. In 2008 language, her offerings, and her brand promise.

Apple's App Store Case Study 2: Atimi Software

Atimi Software is a team of premium mobile app developers. They have an amazing origin story. Founded in 2000 they quickly became, Apple knocked on their door requesting them to build three of the first 100 apps in. After success with Apple, they went off to build mobile apps for the NHL, CFL, NBA, Bloomberg, and many other Fortune 100 companies. They expanded fast, but when the economy worsened, their business suffered significantly. They had to cut over half of their staff and return to operating with a smaller team.

I met them in 2020. The core leadership team shared their future vision and concerns for never landing on marketing collateral that they felt was really "them." They wanted to ramp-up growth; therefore, it was pertinent to build materials that they were proud of and felt represented them well. So, we got to work!

When we got to the ONE IDEA exercise, these were the answers they produced:

Connection

Rescue

Solutions

Job security

Predictability

Simplicity

Ease

Transformation

Comfort

Assurance

Peace of mind

Satisfaction

Achievement

The concept of Peace of Mind resonated with all the leaders. They agreed that their main promise to clients is to bring ease, contentment, and calm to their lives and businesses. That was the moment we knew we had found our core idea.

From there, we interviewed a handful of their clients to ensure we had landed on the correct ONE IDEA. Once they were sure, we went on to create their tagline: Apps done right, the copy and design of the website, including videos to demonstrate their projects.

Their next project is to implement their strategic plan, centered on their ONE IDEA, primarily aimed at enhancing their company culture. Like Simon Sinek said, "Customers will never love a company until the employees love it first."

This is precisely why uncovering the ONE IDEA was paramount. It enables focus to be directed effectively, rallying everyone around a single, impactful philosophy. With a connected and engaged culture, the Atimi team can unite, be rooted in a sense of belonging, and propel their vision and legacy forward.

Incorporating Your ONE IDEA into Your Brand's Narrative

When it comes to defining and expressing your brand, the concept of your ONE IDEA takes center stage. This is not just a marketing strategy; it's the soul of your brand's story. Here are six ways this 1 idea can be woven into the very fabric of your brand's narrative, from your tagline to your social media presence, to cultivating legacy.

Crafting Your Tagline: A tagline is more than a catchy phrase; it is a distilled expression of your brand's essence. Consider Apple's "Think Different" or Coca-Cola's "Open Happiness." These are not just slogans; they are reflections of the companies' core beliefs and values. When developing your tagline, get into the heart of your ONE IDEA. Ensure that your tagline resonates with the transformative value your brand promises to deliver.

Articulating Your Positioning Statement: The first thing visitors encounter on your website is not a detailed history of your company; it is your positioning statement. This statement should be a beacon, guiding them through the fog of the internet directly to your brand. It should succinctly encapsulate who you help, how you help them, and the ultimate outcome of your service. This is not just about being seen; it is about being understood within the blink of an eye.

Refining Your Messaging: Your brand's messaging, whether found on your website, in blog posts, or across social media platforms, should be a reflection of your ONE IDEA. These messages should be succinct, impactful, and unmistakably yours. They should echo the core themes of your brand, making every word count in the grand narrative of what you stand for.

Designing Your Website: Websites are digital kingdoms, a space where your ONE IDEA should reign supreme. From the overall design to the individual words on the page, everything should tell a part of your story. Clarity, consistency, authenticity, engagement, differentiation, and a clear call to action should be the guiding principles behind your website's content. This is where your brand's narrative unfolds, inviting visitors to step into your world and join your journey.

Compiling Your Sales Kit: Your sales kit is not just a collection of marketing materials; it is the embodiment of your ONE IDEA. It should speak directly to your audience, addressing their needs and aspirations while highlighting the unique benefits of partnering with your brand. This is your chance to make a compelling case, not just for what you do, but for the difference you make.

Engaging on social media: social media offers a unique platform to amplify your brand's voice and extend your narrative. Here, your ONE IDEA should illuminate every post, tweet, and story. It is not merely about promoting products or services; it is about building a legacy. By consistently aligning your content with your core idea, you can forge deeper connections with your audience, inspiring them and, ultimately, leaving a lasting impact.

In weaving your ONE IDEA into the narrative of your brand, you are not just selling a product or a service: you are inviting your audience into a story. A story where they are not just customers, but characters, not just consumers, but contributors to a larger mission. This is the power of a well-articulated ONE IDEA—it transforms your brand from a mere entity into a living, breathing story, one that resonates deeply with those it is meant to serve, a legacy.

When you discover your ONE IDEA, you discover the actual business you are in. My legacy is in helping other create and preserve their legacy. It is my passion, my purpose. Now, go, start promoting your promise – your ONE IDEA.

In a world saturated with options, your ONE IDEA is the beacon that guides your brand through the noise. It's not just a tagline or a marketing gimmick; it's the authentic representation of your values, beliefs, and unique selling proposition.

Dedicating time and energy to uncover and polish your ONE IDEA establishes a brand that not only draws in customers but also creates an enduring legacy. By focusing on your ONE IDEA and embedding it throughout your marketing efforts, you foster relationships that surpass mere sales. These relationships become the cornerstone of widespread influence, enabling your brand to touch lives globally and make a significant mark internationally. This is how your brand transcends the ordinary, crafting a legacy that echoes through time and across communities.

~ Azadeh Yaraghi ~

Azadeh is an insightful brand strategist, marketing expert, thought-provoking speaker, #1 bestselling author, and founder of Gogo Telugo Creatives. With 15+ years of international experience, she has built successful brands and earned several marketing awards along the way. Azadeh is passionate about supporting purpose-driven clients who want to grow their business and ultimately leave behind a positive and lasting legacy.

She works with entrepreneurs and organizations who want to get to the heart of their brand so they can attract their ideal clients, build trust and accelerate growth. She is the past President of the Canadian Association of Professional Speakers (BC Chapter), a proud mentor at Futurpreneur, and an Advisory Board Member for the Healthy Heroes Foundation. In her free time, she enjoys flamenco and salsa dancing, playing beach volleyball, and taking long walks along the seawall in spectacular Vancouver.

~ Chapter 5 ~

Melody Woods

Making Every Moment Matter

It is easy to feel overwhelmed when making decisions about your health or well-being in a world brimming with information and choices. From managing stress to achieving optimal fitness, navigating the sea of health advice can be daunting. Yet, it is these very decisions that sculpt our legacy, shaping how we live and how we are remembered. By prioritizing our health, we not only enhance our daily lives but also set a foundation for a legacy of vitality, resilience, and well-being. Making informed choices leads to a life lived with intention and purpose, reflecting our deepest values and aspirations.

What would my legacy be?

I began my professional business career at the age of sixteen, studying all aspects of running a business. From operations, management, administration, accounting, manufacturing, sales, marketing, ecommerce, and more, I was learning how to think quickly on my feet, get the job done, find solutions to problems never seen, develop processes, and leave no stone unchecked.

When I thought of legacy during this time frame of my late teens to early twenties, I focused on acquiring skills and thought processes needed for building my legacy, but I still had no clue what that would be.

As I navigated through the complexities of each role, I began to understand that legacy is not just about the knowledge acquired or the success achieved; it is about the impact made on others and the contributions to the community. It dawned on me that building a legacy was more than just personal achievement; it was about creating something that lasts beyond one's lifetime, influencing future generations and leaving a positive imprint on the world. This realization was the turning point, guiding my actions and decisions towards a more purposeful path.

The next time I thought about legacy was when I was first diagnosed with cancer at 26. After all the recent firsts in my life: newly married, new house, and now cancer, my thought of legacy turned to what I was going to leave behind. I still had nothing. I felt like I had not lived yet and only knew illness by caring for and being around sick loved ones for the past 14 years. Watching my sick loved ones battle their various autoimmune conditions and health battles gave this young kid a different perspective when it was my turn to face one of my biggest battles, cancer. I saw from a child's perspective that the sick got sicker.

I remember staying the night one weekend with my grandma to help her out when I was twelve. I asked that evening during dinner why she had certain magazines and topics pinned, as she mentioned that she was educating herself on things that she felt were related to her health. My curiosity about the root cause had developed at a young age from this moment with my grandma. She believed her symptoms were connected, but she was not sure what she was missing in her health. I love the fact that my curiosity at such a young age prompted me to have this conversation with her, as it was a profound moment I reflected on during my health journey.

I researched and educated myself on all cancers, looking for common protocols and health patterns, and started to look for clues on why all the women in my family were so sick. I took a hybrid approach of traditional medicine and alternative treatments in the early days.

One of the approaches I chose was natural treatments to support my body. Working with doctors and following some of the alternative protocols I had read about in the various cancer books helped strengthen my foundation. Choosing the path with alternative treatments along with surgery came from the deep-seated, nagging feeling that I would not make it if I chose the standard course. I did not know why I felt so powerfully strong in this stance until many years later something that I teach about listening to your health intuition.

Listen quietly to the signals your body gives to the things you encounter, whether those be people, your internal and external environment, food, or products. It felt like instinct. This instinct of supporting my body naturally gave me more time. I was armed with information I would reflect on later in life because of this path.

This profound journey into the depths of my own health challenges led me to a deeper understanding of life's fragility and the importance of each moment. Embracing this new perspective, I began to see the value in every interaction and the potential to make a meaningful difference. My approach to life shifted from merely surviving to thriving, with a focus on creating positive impacts wherever I went. This period of introspection and personal growth was instrumental in shaping my approach to legacy, teaching me that it's not just about leaving something behind, but also about the quality of presence and the positive influence we exert in the lives of others every day.

While living with cancer for 18 years, over the course of each year, I was trying to find ways to buy more time, save more time, and do more each day, knowing my time was probably limited, making sure I gave more of myself to those I came in contact with whether they knew the depths of the health challenges I faced or not. My legacy during this time was enriching people's lives with the problems I could solve in business.

The knowledge I gained from seeing, learning, and experiencing an integrative approach to medicine early on helped me forge the path I needed when plagued with a trifecta of health conditions in 2018 while still with cancer in the background. Leaving the hospital just a few hours later, left miserable and feeling even closer to death, I took matters into my own hands as I waited for a doctor to get medicine, which was weeks out knowing that waiting for medical care to be seen shortened your chances for quality of life. There was no way I was sitting on the sidelines, potentially losing a job, house, and all things in my life that I had fought so hard to maintain during 15 years of cancer at this point. I have also built a resilient mindset, learning how to reinvent myself. So, these health challenges were no different.

I went back to that same curiosity I had as a kid; when I asked my grandma why she kept magazines, Immediately I dug out my stack of articles, treatments from the past, and books. I started looking for my connection to what I might have missed over the years again. What I felt so strongly about then and still now is that I started to find ways to support those health conditions naturally.

All the years I spent, as a teen and adult around entrepreneurs, leaders, managers, those who got things done, and found solutions to problems where there were no processes or measurements, I had developed the perfect skillset I used each day that prepared me for this moment to change the conversation of health and seek out answers to the tough questions or to ask the question that had never been asked and find the solutions and steps I needed to regain my health.

My unorthodox approach combining traditional and alternative treatments so many years ago had me double down with these new conditions I fell upon. If there was another possible chance of even more cancer in my thyroid, or perhaps needing surgery first for large fibroids, being anemic, and close to needing a blood transfusion as my body worked harder than ever to keep me alive, I had nothing to lose. This provided a realization that my timeline to get things done (that I wanted) and to achieve was sped up.

It was time to take action.

Since I had seen so much illness as a child, I started asking different questions when it related to my health—different questions to the doctors and different questions to myself. If a doctor did not have a solution, I looked for one. I was asking what new medical information, studies, and researchers had discovered that related to any of my health conditions or my family conditions, and the stack of articles and pages pinned in books looking to see any new developments or connections now existed where there once weren't—looking at ways to support my body once again.

I trusted the fact that I would find a solution and make the connections; the only question of doubt was, again, time. Would I have enough time to reverse the damage done to my body from these conditions?

This relentless pursuit of answers and solutions became a defining aspect of my journey, reinforcing my belief in the power of proactive health management. As I navigated through the maze of medical information and alternative therapies, I became more attuned to my body's needs and the subtle signals it was sending. This deepened sense of self-awareness and commitment to my health empowered me to advocate for myself in ways I never had before. It was a testament to the strength and resilience that had been forged through years of adversity. This period of intense self-advocacy and research was not just about finding a cure; it was about reclaiming control over my life and health, ensuring that every decision aligned with my ultimate goal: to live a life defined by purpose, vitality, and a legacy of resilience.

Now, in business, you base your financial decisions on numbers and facts. Therefore, I started to follow the basics of medical science. Similarly, like you would tackle a business problem, could the information I found on my conditions or symptoms be tested and measured? If so, how? Did anyone succeed in doing this, or had they looked at these conditions or symptoms from the health questions I was looking for an answer to?

I was not only looking to help buy more time and enrich the lives of others over this period, but secretly, I was building my immunity and slowly repairing the years of damage, repairing my foundation due to the choices I was making, combining alternative medicine once again but incorporating all the business skills of problem-solving over these.

This approach to my health was akin to a strategic business review, where every aspect is scrutinized, and every strategy is evaluated for its efficacy. Just as a business must adapt to the changing market, I learned that my approach to health must be dynamic and responsive to the changing needs of my body. This realization was empowering, as it underscored the importance of agility and adaptability, not just in business, but in life and health as well.

The complexity of your health problems is intertwined with various systems of your body. Providing support for those systems is key to feeling optimal and well again. When you face health challenges for any duration, doctors, family, and friends are quick to tell you to stop living. As a person facing these health challenges for any duration, you realize that life does stop.

However, I refused to accept this cessation of life as my fate. Instead, I chose to view each challenge as an opportunity for growth and learning. This mindset shift was crucial, transforming despair into determination and passivity into action. It was a testament to the power of a positive outlook, which, when combined with informed, strategic actions, can lead to remarkable outcomes.

My health strategies led to greater healing time, heading off illnesses before they took hold, newfound energy, and resilience when I used to have none. I even beat cancer after 18 years because I had the tools and skillset from business and all the information, I had gathered over the years to see how the pieces fit relating to my health.

Due to other people's legacies that they had built, the knowledge and skillset they developed on health who were willing to share their discoveries in books, seminars, and teachings, I was able to discover and forge and develop my immunity and path for the legacy I live behind.

We hear all the time that food is medicine, but no one teaches us how it works and how it relates to us personally. We also hear if you are doing alternative treatments that, everything is connected, yet again, no one teaches us how they relate to your health.

This gap in our understanding and education around health and wellness is where my journey takes on a new dimension. It became clear that the conventional approach to health, while effective for some, was not the complete answer for everyone. The realization that there is no one-size-fits-all solution to health challenges led me to explore and embrace a more holistic approach. This exploration was not just about treating symptoms but understanding and addressing the root causes of illness.

By integrating the wisdom of traditional medicine with the innovative approaches of alternative therapies, I began to see significant improvements in my health. This journey was not without its trials and errors, but each step brought me closer to understanding the unique needs of my body and how to meet them. It taught me the importance of personalized health care — recognizing that every individual's path to wellness is unique and requires a tailored approach.

Moreover, this journey illuminated the interconnectedness of mind, body, and spirit. I learned that mental and emotional well-being are just as important as physical health, and that all three are deeply interconnected.

This holistic view of health has not only been transformative for me personally but has also shaped the advice and support I offer to others.

As I unlocked my healthcare mysteries, I discovered and felt healthy like never before and discovered the legacy I would leave behind. A legacy of strength, knowledge, and guidance to those facing health challenges to ask a different question: how are you changing the conversation of your health?

This legacy is not just about surviving; it is about thriving. It is about moving beyond the traditional narratives of health and illness and forging a new path that embraces the full spectrum of well-being. My journey has taught me that by changing the conversation around health, by asking different questions, and by being open to new possibilities, we can transform our lives. This is the legacy I aim to leave behind — a testament to the power of self-advocacy, the importance of personalized health solutions, and the transformative potential of holistic well-being.

~ Melody Woods ~

Melody is recognized as one of the most requested in-demand coaches and motivational keynote speakers in health and wellness, high performance, and business. She is the behind-the-scenes, go-to advisor for many top business professionals, entrepreneurs, and thought leaders in business, as well as an educator on autoimmune or chronic illnesses, teaching anyone who wants to get more done, be more, feel better how to leverage their knowledge and resources, trust their intuition, and live life despite the hand they are dealt with their health and body

Meet Melody, a dedicated and passionate health, life and business coach who has dedicated her life to helping others transform and reach their fullest potential. With a deep-rooted commitment to holistic wellness, Melody empowers individuals to take charge of their physical, mental, and emotional health, guiding them on a transformative journey towards a more vibrant and fulfilling life personally and professionally.

She is the behind-the-scenes, go-to advisor for many top business professionals, entrepreneurs, and thought leaders in business as well as an educator on autoimmune or chronic illnesses, teaching anyone who wants to get more done, be more, feel better how to leverage their knowledge and resources, and trust their intuition. With a wealth of knowledge, a compassionate heart, and a proven track record of success, Melody is the trusted partner you need on your path to a healthier, happier, and more balanced life of success.

~ Chapter 6 ~

CAROLYN RUBIN

Illuminating Healthcare: An Enduring Legacy

In the area of healthcare, where my compassion converges with innovation, I have been blessed to learn what I have and truly embrace its lessons. Over three decades, I have emerged, beginning as a pharmacy technician then onward to become a beacon of inspiration and transformation in the healthcare landscape. My journey has become a testament to unwavering dedication, resilience, and visionary leadership.

My journey began within the confines of the pharmacy. It was here, in the heart of healthcare delivery, that my passion for serving others began to take shape. As a pharmacy technician, I immersed myself in the intricacies of medication management and patient care, meticulously filling prescriptions and providing vital support to those in need.

In this environment, I honed my skills and developed a deep understanding of the crucial role that pharmacists and pharmacy technicians play in the healthcare system. I witnessed firsthand the profound impact that compassionate care and attention to detail can have on patients' well-being. Whether I was assisting a worried parent with a sick child or providing medication counseling to an elderly patient, I recognized the importance of empathy, communication, and expertise in delivering quality healthcare services.

It was within the pharmacy walls that my commitment to healing, and advocacy began to take root. Every interaction, no matter how routine, served as a reminder of the profound responsibility that healthcare professionals carry—the responsibility to alleviate suffering, promote wellness, and advocate for those in their care. My experiences as pharmacy technician laid the foundation for my future endeavors, instilling in me a deep-seated dedication to making a difference in the lives of others.

As I navigated the challenges and rewards of my role, my passion for serving others only grew stronger. I witnessed the transformative power of compassionate healthcare delivery, and I knew that I wanted to play a larger role in shaping the future of the industry. Little did I know that my journey from the pharmacy shelves to the forefront of healthcare innovation was just beginning.

Driven by my desire to make a more significant impact on the healthcare landscape, I embarked on a journey to become a certified medical assistant. Recognizing the importance of bridging the gap between patients and healthcare providers, I sought to expand my skill set and enhance my ability to deliver compassionate care. My role as a pharmacy technician taught me how important patient care was, regardless of the delivery (Pharmacy vs bedside as an example). Through rigorous training and dedication, I earned my certification, paving the way for a new chapter in my career.

As a certified medical assistant, I became a crucial link in the chain of healthcare delivery. My role encompassed a diverse range of responsibilities, from assisting physicians during examinations to performing vital sign measurements and administering medications. However, it was my innate ability to connect with patients on a deeper level that truly set me apart.

With empathy and compassion as my guiding principles, I approached each interaction with sincerity and care. I took the time to listen to patients' concerns, address their questions, and alleviate their fears. Whether I was comforting a nervous patient before a procedure or providing education on medication management, my unwavering dedication to my patients' well-being shone through.

In addition to my clinical duties, I also took on the role of advocate for my patients. I recognized that many individuals faced barriers to accessing quality healthcare, from financial constraints to language barriers, and at times due to cultural differences. I tirelessly advocated for my patients' rights and ensured that they received the care and support they deserved.

As those 'important people' began to recognize my exemplary work ethic and commitment to excellence, I earned a reputation as a healthcare trailblazer. My colleagues and patients alike recognized me as a trusted ally and advocate, someone who could be relied upon to deliver exceptional care with integrity and compassion. My ability to empathize with patients and my tireless advocacy for their well-being cemented my legacy as a true champion of healthcare.

I embraced my role as a speaker, stepping onto stages with confidence and conviction, using my platform to inspire and ignite change. With a wealth of knowledge and experience at my disposal, I captivated audiences with my insights and perspectives, shedding light on pressing issues and challenging the status quo.

Through my speaking engagements, I sought to empower the next generation of healthcare professionals, instilling in them the values of compassion and excellence. Drawing from my own journey, I shared practical wisdom and real-world experiences, equipping my audience with the tools they needed to succeed in their own careers. Whether addressing a room full of medical students or seasoned professionals, my passion for mentorship and education shone through, leaving a lasting impression on all who had the privilege of hearing me speak.

In addition to my work as a speaker, I also made a significant impact through my writing. As a prolific author, my words became a force for transformation, advocating for patient rights, ethical practices, and innovation within the healthcare industry. Through articles, blog posts, and op-eds, I tackled a wide range of topics, from healthcare policy and legislation to the latest advancements in medical technology.

My writing not only informed and educated but also inspired and provoked critical thinking, sparking dialogue and driving progress within healthcare. I learned how to distill complex concepts into accessible language and compelling narratives which made me a trusted voice within the industry, and my work served as a catalyst for positive change.

Whether I was speaking from a stage or penning a new article, my passion for making a difference in the lives of others was palpable. My dedication to advocating for patient rights and promoting excellence in healthcare set me apart as a true leader and innovator. With my speaking engagements and writing endeavors, I wielded the power to inspire, inform, and transform, leaving an indelible mark on healthcare across numerous departments.

Championing patient advocacy and servant leadership, I assumed the mantle of a patient advocate, embodying the values of empathy, compassion, and advocacy. With a keen ear and a compassionate heart, I listened intently to the concerns and needs of patients, providing a comforting presence in times of uncertainty and distress. My ability to empathize with patients and understand their unique circumstances allowed me to champion their cause with unwavering dedication and resolve.

My reach extended far beyond mere titles or job descriptions; it became ingrained in every aspect of my life. As a servant leader, I embraced the philosophy of putting others first, prioritizing collaboration, empathy, and growth in all my interactions. Regardless of working alongside colleagues in a healthcare team or mentoring aspiring professionals, I sought to uplift and empower those around me, recognizing that true leadership is about serving others.

In my role as a servant leader, I fostered a culture of collaboration and mutual respect, where all individual's contributions were valued and celebrated. I encouraged open communication and dialogue, creating an environment where ideas could flourish, and innovation could thrive. Through my example, I inspired others to lead with integrity, compassion, and a relentless commitment to serving the needs of patients above all else.

With unwavering dedication to serving others becoming the cornerstone of my legacy, leaving an indelible mark on the hearts and minds of all who had the privilege of knowing me became something I strived for. My leadership style, characterized by humility, empathy, and a genuine concern for others' well-being, I realized that I inspired countless individuals to follow in my footsteps and embrace the principles of servant leadership in their own lives and careers.

As my journey progresses, my legacy as a compassionate advocate and servant leader will continue to expand, serving as a guiding light for future generations of healthcare professionals. Through my selfless dedication to serving others, I have left an imprint on the healthcare landscape, reminding us of all the transformative power that empathy, compassion, and servant leadership bring.

My journey underwent a profound transformation when I took pen to paper and shared my story in the anthology "You Can Overcome Anything." In these pages, readers discover that narrative of resilience, courage, and triumph—a testament to my indomitable spirit and unwavering determination in the face of adversity. My words offered solace and inspiration to individuals navigating their own challenges, reminding them that no obstacle is insurmountable with perseverance and courage.

Still, my impact extends beyond the written word. Through my media appearances on platforms such as CUTV News, T.I.P. Radio, and the Frank McKay Show, I can amplify my message, reaching audiences far and wide with my story of hope and empowerment. Whether sharing personal anecdotes, discussing pressing healthcare issues, or offering words of encouragement, my authenticity and passion resonated with listeners, leaving a lasting impression on all who had the privilege of hearing me speak.

Through my storytelling and advocacy, I became a beacon of hope for those grappling with adversity, a guiding light illuminating the path to resilience and triumph. My willingness to share my own struggles and triumphs served as a source of inspiration and empowerment for countless individuals, reminding them of their own strength and resilience in the face of life's challenges.

As a contributor to esteemed publications such as Beckers, American Health & Information Management Association (AHIMA), and AAPC (American Association of Professional Coders), I wielded my pen as a powerful instrument for change within the healthcare industry. Through my articles, I shared invaluable insights and expertise with a global audience, offering practical wisdom and guidance to medical assisting students, physicians, and healthcare professionals alike.

My articles were more than just words on a page; they became beacons of knowledge and inspiration, illuminating the path toward excellence in healthcare delivery. With a keen understanding of the complexities and challenges facing the industry, I provided readers with actionable strategies and best practices aimed at improving patient care, enhancing operational efficiency, and driving innovation.

My impact reaches beyond the pages of prestigious publications. Through my efforts, I played a pivotal role in certifying over 2500 AAPC coders, equipping them with the skills and knowledge needed to excel in their roles and contribute to the advancement of the healthcare landscape. My commitment to excellence and dedication to shaping the future of healthcare left a mark on the industry's landscape, ensuring that my legacy will endure for generations to come.

As my contributions continue to shape the healthcare industry, my influence serves as a testament to the transformative power of knowledge, mentorship, and advocacy. Through my work as a writer and educator, I empowered countless individuals to strive for excellence and innovation in their own pursuits, leaving an enduring legacy of impact and inspiration.

As an Executive Contributor for Brainz Magazine and a Contributing Author for Passion Vista Magazine, I transcended geographical boundaries to share my vision for a better healthcare ecosystem with global audiences. Through these prestigious platforms, I leveraged my expertise and insight to advocate for positive change within the healthcare industry, inspiring others to join me in shaping a brighter future for healthcare worldwide.

My leadership and mentorship were not only recognized but celebrated in publications such as, Who's Who of the Industries, Brilliance Magazine, and Voices of Women. These accolades solidified my status as a thought leader in my field, affirming my influence and impact on the healthcare landscape.

Through my contributions to these esteemed publications, I sparked important conversations that drove meaningful change on a global scale. Whether discussing emerging healthcare trends, advocating for patient rights, or championing innovative solutions to healthcare challenges, my voice resonated with audiences around the world, inspiring them to action and igniting a collective movement toward a more equitable, compassionate, and sustainable healthcare ecosystem.

My influence transcended boundaries, bridging the gap between different cultures, languages, and perspectives. My unwavering commitment to driving positive change and my dedication to advancing healthcare for all solidified my legacy as a transformative leader and visionary within the industry. As my impact continues to ripple outward, my contributions will serve as a beacon of inspiration for generations to come, inspiring others to follow in my footsteps and make a difference in the world of healthcare.

The International Association of Women bestowed upon me a series of prestigious awards that not only recognized my influence and leadership but also celebrated my unwavering commitment to making a difference in the healthcare industry. As the recipient of awards such as Top Healthcare Executive of the Year, Empowered Woman of the Year, and Most Inspirational Woman of the Year, my dedication and contributions were honored on a global stage.

My name graced the Nasdaq Billboard in New York City, symbolizing my unquenchable spirit and enduring impact in the healthcare industry. This momentous recognition served as a testament to my relentless pursuit of excellence and my tireless advocacy for positive change within the healthcare landscape.

My legacy as a fearless leader and advocate for change I hope will continue to inspire generations to come. With remarkable achievements and accolades serving as a beacon of hope and empowerment, I hope to motivate others to strive for greatness and make a meaningful impact in their own spheres of influence.

As my journey unfolds and my legacy endures, my name will remain synonymous with innovation, compassion, and transformative leadership within the healthcare industry. My extraordinary contributions have left an indelible mark on the hearts and minds of all who have had the privilege of knowing me, inspiring countless individuals to follow in my footsteps and continue the work of shaping a brighter future for healthcare.

As each day draws to a close, my legacy continues to radiate with increasing brilliance, serving as a guiding light for leaders of today and tomorrow. My journey inspires countless individuals to embrace the principles of compassion, innovation, and servant leadership in their own endeavors.

My unwavering commitment to making a difference in the lives of others has left a mark on the healthcare industry and beyond. Through my dedication to serving and as a beacon of inspiration, I have empowered countless individuals to pursue excellence and strive for positive change in their respective fields.

As I continue to share my passion, leadership, and mentorship through platforms such as my TV show, EmpowerFuse: 'Unleashing Inspiration Together,' my legacy will endure as a guiding light in the ever-evolving landscape of healthcare. My commitment to uplifting and empowering others ensures that my impact will be felt for generations to come, inspiring future leaders to follow in my footsteps and continue the journey toward a brighter, more compassionate future for all.

~ Carolyn Rubin ~

Carolyn Rubin is a seasoned healthcare professional, author, and inspirational speaker dedicated to transforming the landscape of healthcare through compassion and innovation. With over three decades of experience, Carolyn began her journey as a pharmacy technician, where she cultivated her passion for patient care and advocacy. As a certified medical assistant, she bridged the gap between patients and providers, ensuring seamless communication and compassionate care. Carolyn's leadership extends beyond titles, embodying servant leadership principles to uplift and empower those around her.

A prolific writer and speaker, she amplifies voices, advocates for patient rights, and fosters dialogue within the healthcare community. Carolyn's legacy of fearless leadership continues to inspire generations to embrace compassion, innovation, and servant leadership in their own pursuits. Through her TV show, EmpowerFuse 'Unleashing Inspiration Together,' she shares her passion, leadership, and mentorship, ensuring her legacy endures as a guiding light in the ever-evolving landscape of healthcare

~ Chapter 7 ~
JONI B. REDICK-YUNDT
The Million Dollar Journey: Cultivating Resilience, Empowering Dreams, Creating Legacy

In a world teeming with unique stories of success and resilience, mine weaves through the vibrant array of life's vast experiences, guided by what I have come to know as the Million Dollar Attitude. This is not merely a philosophy but the essence of my life's journey—from my humble beginnings in the Philippines to achieving dreams I once thought were beyond reach. It represents a profound truth…

Our destiny is not just shaped by the circumstances we encounter but by how we choose to navigate them.

With a belief in the power of attitude, action, and altruism, I have carved a path that transcends boundaries, touching lives, and empowering spirits along the way. As I share this narrative, it unfolds the chapters of my life, each marked by challenges overcome, dreams realized, and lessons learned. It is a testament to the power of positivity, the importance of perseverance, and the immeasurable impact of leading with love and empathy. This journey, my legacy, is anchored in the Million Dollar Attitude—a comprehensive guide to living a life filled with purpose, passion, and profound impact.

In the process of creating what has become my legacy, the principles that have guided me are encapsulated in a book I wrote called "The Million Dollar Attitude." This philosophy though is not just a mantra; it is a blueprint for achieving success and fulfillment in life. Each letter of this phrase represents a key to unlocking one's potential and navigating the complexities of our existence with grace, determination, and positivity.

THE MILLION DOLLAR ATTITUDE

My journey begins with the humility of my early years, where the seeds of this attitude were unknowingly sown. The "M" in Million stands for "Make things happen." From the bustling streets of the Philippines to the diverse landscapes of Hawaii, I learned the value of initiative and the power of turning dreams into reality. It was here, amid adversity, that I learned the true meaning of resilience, the essence of making things happen against all odds.

The "I" represents "Imagine and visualize your dreams." As a young girl, my dreams were vivid, but the path to achieving them was obscured by my circumstances. Yet, I dared to imagine a future beyond my immediate reality. This imaginative spirit propelled me forward, guiding me through my academic advancements and into the realms of nursing and entrepreneurship. Imagining my dreams was the first step in a journey of a thousand miles—a journey marked by achievements, learning, and growth.

"Love one another," the first "L" in Million, embodies my foundational belief in compassion and empathy. This principle shone brightly throughout my nursing career, serving as a guiding light toward forming genuine connections and delivering impactful service. It's a testament to the profound influence that compassion can have, not only on those we serve but on our own lives, enriching each interaction with warmth and understanding.

"Live a life of serenity," the second "L," has been a vital principle in navigating the ebbs and flows of my journey. This ethos guided me through the storms, serving as a constant reminder of the importance of maintaining inner peace and balance amidst life's inevitable chaos. It underscores the value of seeking tranquility in our lives, fostering an environment where both the mind and spirit can flourish.

"Initiate action," another "I," became my mantra as I transitioned from healthcare to the financial sector. Recognizing the need for financial literacy and security in the wake of personal loss, I took decisive steps to empower others through education and support. This initiative laid the groundwork for FAMES Hawaii, embodying my commitment to action and change.

"Open your mind," represented by "O," echoes my journey of constant learning and adaptation. From the shores of the Philippines to the diverse cultural landscape of Hawaii, and through the various sectors I've navigated, keeping an open mind has been crucial. This openness has fostered innovation, growth, and an inclusive approach to leadership and mentorship.

"Never quit - embrace adversity," encapsulated by "N," is a powerful testament to the resilience that has been both my shield and my compass throughout life's journey. This principle has taught me to confront challenges with unwavering determination, transforming each obstacle into a stepping stone toward greater achievements. From the initial hurdles of cultural assimilation as an immigrant, grappling with a new language, customs, and often, a sense of isolation, to the rigorous trials encountered in the high-stakes arenas of my professional life, each instance of adversity has been a classroom. These experiences have ingrained in me a profound understanding of perseverance's true value and the undeniable strength that emerges when we choose to face our battles head-on. Embracing adversity, instead of avoiding it, has not only shaped my character but has also illuminated the path to resilience, teaching me that the essence of true strength lies in the courage to continue, even when the odds seem insurmountable.

"Dare to live," the "D" in Dollar, reflects my approach to life and career. Whether leaping into the financial services industry, embarking on philanthropic endeavors with FAMES Hawaii, or exploring the realms of luxury design, I've lived by the credo of daring to live fully, passionately, and purposefully.

"Organize," the "O" in DOLLAR, is a principle that has been instrumental in my journey. The ability to organize not only my thoughts and plans but also the environments and teams around me has been crucial. Whether it was structuring my day-to-day activities to make room for both my career and my passions or arranging complex financial solutions for clients, the organization has been the backbone of efficiency and effectiveness. It's about creating a clear path towards our goals, ensuring that every action is intentional, and every effort is aligned with our ultimate objectives. This organizational prowess has enabled me to navigate the multifaceted aspects of my career and personal endeavors with clarity and purpose, turning visions into realities.

"Live life to the fullest," the first "L" in DOLLAR, encapsulates my philosophy towards life. This isn't just about embracing every moment with enthusiasm but also about seeking out those experiences that enrich our souls, challenge our perceptions, and elevate our understanding of the world and ourselves. Living life to the fullest means diving headfirst into the opportunities that life offers, whether it's through professional growth, personal exploration, or contributing to the betterment of society through philanthropic efforts. It's a commitment to experiencing life in its entirety, savoring the joys, navigating the sorrows, and emerging with a deeper appreciation for the journey.

"Learn and grow," the second "L" in DOLLAR, underscores the importance of continuous personal and professional development. My life's path has been marked by an insatiable curiosity and a relentless pursuit of knowledge. From the earliest days of my career in nursing to the challenges of the financial world, and through the creative realms of design and entrepreneurship, each step has been a learning opportunity. This principle is about embracing every chance to expand our horizons and understanding that growth is a perpetual journey. It's through this lens of lifelong learning that I've been able to adapt, innovate, and lead with insight, recognizing that each lesson learned is a cornerstone in the edifice of a fulfilling life.

"Act on your dreams, do not procrastinate," represented by "A" in DOLLAR, speaks to the dynamic force of action in the realization of our ambitions. Dreaming is the first step, but it's the courage to act on those dreams that transforms them into reality. My journey has been characterized by taking decisive steps toward my goals, whether it was leaping into a new career, launching a nonprofit organization, or venturing into new creative industries. This principle is a clarion call to move beyond the comfort zone, to set plans into motion, and to embrace the beauty of starting—even when the outcome is uncertain. It's a reminder that the perfect time is now and that the dreams we dare to act upon are the ones that define our legacy.

"Resourceful and get results," represented by "R," has been a guiding principle in my endeavors. Whether navigating the complexities of the financial industry, spearheading initiatives with FAMES Hawaii, or diving into the realms of luxury design and authorship, resourcefulness has been key to overcoming obstacles and achieving tangible outcomes. This trait has empowered me to find innovative solutions to challenges, turning potential setbacks into opportunities for growth and success.

Most important, is the ATTITUDE taken when creating a legacy. The "A" stands for "Absorb knowledge and wisdom." My journey across continents, careers, and cultures has been underpinned by an insatiable appetite for learning. From the academic rigors of my early education to the practical insights gained through my varied professional experiences, absorbing knowledge and wisdom has been crucial. It's a continuous process that enriches the mind, fuels innovation, and fosters empathy, enabling me to lead with insight and compassion.

"Take it to the top," the first "T," encapsulates my approach to ambition and achievement. It's not just about setting goals but aspiring to reach the zenith in every endeavor. This principle has driven me to excel in my financial career, establish and grow FAMES Hawaii into a beacon of mentorship and support, and venture into the competitive world of luxury fashion with confidence and vision.

"Teamwork," another "T," underscores the importance of collaboration in realizing one's dreams. The successes I've celebrated, from early accolades in the financial sector to the impactful work done through FAMES Hawaii, have been collective achievements. Teamwork has enabled me to amplify my impact, bringing together diverse talents and perspectives towards common goals. It's a reminder that together, we can achieve more than we ever could alone.

"Inspire others," the final "I," is perhaps the most profound aspect of the Million Dollar Attitude. My journey has been about more than personal achievement; it's been a platform to uplift, motivate, and inspire others. From mentoring young entrepreneurs and students to sharing my story through speaking engagements and my books, inspiring others has been at the heart of my mission. It's about lighting a spark in others and encouraging them to pursue their dreams with courage and conviction.

"Together we can do it," the last "T," reinforces the message of unity and collective effort. Whether it's through FAMES Hawaii, my speaking engagements, or my personal interactions, I've witnessed the incredible power of collective action. This principle is a call to action, urging us to join hands in pursuit of a better world, where dreams are realized, challenges are surmounted, and success is shared.

"Undaunted; perfectionism is paralysis," represented by "U," speaks to the courage required to pursue one's goals in the face of uncertainty and the pitfalls of striving for unattainable perfection. It's a reminder to

embrace imperfection as part of the growth process, to be bold in the pursuit of one's passions, and to remain steadfast in the face of adversity.

"Don't be sensitive or defensive," the "D" in Attitude, emphasizes the importance of openness to feedback and constructive criticism. It's a call to approach challenges and differences of opinion with grace, seeing them as opportunities for growth and understanding rather than threats.

Finally, "Energetic, excited, enthusiastic; exercise and have fun," the concluding "E," captures the essence of living a life filled with joy, passion, and vitality. It's about approaching each day with enthusiasm, finding joy in the journey, and embracing a lifestyle that balances hard work with the importance of fun and self-care.

The Million Dollar Attitude spelled out through these guiding principles, is more than a formula for success; it's a way of life. It embodies the journey I've undertaken, the lessons I've learned, and the legacy I aim to leave behind. It's a roadmap for anyone aspiring to lead a life marked by achievement, purpose, and joy. Let this philosophy guide us as we navigate the complexities of life, aiming always to make a positive impact, inspire others, and achieve our fullest potential. Together, with a Million Dollar Attitude, we can transform our lives and the world around us.

This philosophy, the Million Dollar Attitude, has been the cornerstone of my journey and my legacy. It is woven into every endeavor I've undertaken, every challenge I've faced, and every achievement I've celebrated. It is a testament to the transformative power of attitude, belief, and action—a blueprint for living a life of purpose, impact, and fulfillment.

As I reflect on my journey, I am reminded of the indelible impact of these principles. They are not just abstract concepts but lived experiences, lessons learned, and wisdom gained. They are the legacy I wish to leave behind—a legacy of empowerment, transformation, and unwavering positivity. With the Million Dollar Attitude as our guide, we can navigate the complexities of life, achieve our highest aspirations, and inspire those around us to do the same.

Integrating the narratives of overcoming early life challenges, embracing the ethos of resilience, and building a legacy through empowerment and inspiration, this reflection encapsulates the essence of a life lived with a Million Dollar Attitude. It's a testament to the power of positivity, the importance of perseverance, and the immeasurable impact of leading with love and empathy, setting a path for others to follow.

~ JONI B. REDICK-YUNDT~

Joni B. Redick-Yundt, celebrated for her Million Dollar Attitude, has excelled internationally as a Financial Professional and entrepreneur for nearly 30 years. Starting her career with distinctions like Rookie of the Year and Million Dollar Round Table membership, she now leads Names Hawaii as CEO/Founder.

An international best-selling author and motivational speaker, Joni also owns a luxury handbag brand, which includes jewelry and fragrance. Her leadership and philanthropy earned her the Top Influential Business & Community Leader award in 2021 by IAOTP, among other accolades like Empowered Woman of the Year 2022. Joni also is the owner of a limousine service and carries roles as an executive TV producer, host, and so much more.

A cancer survivor, Joni's resilience extends beyond her professional achievements. Her most famed is as a devoted mother & grandmother, and wife. Joni's amazing journey showcases her diverse talents and unwavering pursuit of excellence.

~ Chapter 8 ~
CRYSTAL L. PRIVETT
A Legacy of Hope

Envision a world where your legacy transcends the constraints of fear and abandonment, guiding you towards a life that is not only heart-centered but also rich in spirit, love, and wholeness. This kind of love, perhaps, is the very essence that propels both your professional and personal life to unparalleled heights, benefiting not just yourself but also those around you.

A legacy, in its most profound sense, encompasses far more than the tangible assets we leave behind, it includes our faith, ethics, core values, character, reputation, and the life we lead. Its about setting an example that inspires others to forge their paths with integrity and purpose.

Often, when we contemplate legacy, our minds drift to grandiose visions of empires or wealth destined for future generations. Yet, more frequently than acknowledged, it is our daily actions and character that forge a legacy, impacting those in our lives with the essence of our being. Regardless of whether we inherit material wealth, we all receive and pass on an intangible legacy composed of thoughts, feelings, actions, and behaviors that have shaped us from childhood.

The legacy I inherited was one I determinedly chose not to continue. Its a poignant truth that not all of us are born into a legacy of prosperity, yet we each possess the extraordinary capacity to craft the legacy we envision for ourselves. My journey began from a place of profound vulnerability—before I even took my first breath, my path was shadowed by a legacy of pain and fear.

The moment my mother discovered my gender, a silent battle against a cycle of generational trauma began. Bringing a child into the world is among life's most sacred moments, filled with hopes of nurturing this new soul with love, protection, and the best version of ourselves.

Sharing this story with you is an act of courage, born from a lifetime of seeking healing and connection. My narrative is a testament to the resilience of the human spirit, a journey through darkness towards light, driven by a relentless pursuit of truth and healing. Despite appearing outwardly vibrant and strong, I navigated through life feeling broken, abandoned, and unseen, yearning for love and recognition. Unbeknownst to me, the shadows of my past set the stage fora repetitive cycle of pain, drawing me towards people and situations that echoed the lessons I had yet to learn.

In a society where emotional suppression and stoicism are often valorized, the necessity to confront and integrate our deepest wounds is frequently overlooked. Yet, it is precisely this journey of acknowledgment and healing that led me to a pivotal moment of self-realization. I found myself in a marriage that, rather than nurturing me, perpetuated the cycle of trauma into which I was born. This realization catalyzed a profound transformation, prompting me to choose liberation and healing for myself and my children over the continuation of generational suffering.

Upon the revelation about my forthcoming birth—my fathers declaration of intent to harm me based on my gender—casts a long shadow over my early years. The concept that a parent could premeditate harm to their own child is a chilling testament to the destructive power of unresolved trauma. My fathers actions extended beyond personal sexual transgressions, creating a network of exploitation that exposed me to unimaginable harm. From being used as a pawn in his private human trafficking ring to being exchanged for favors amongst those who should have been protectors, my childhood was marred by betrayal.

These formative years are crucial in shaping our perceptions and beliefs, embedding patterns of thought and behavior that can last a lifetime. Yet, it was within this crucible of suffering that my spirit, resilient and undeterred, began to forge a different path—one of healing, empowerment, and the creation of a new legacy.

This story is not just mine; it is a call to all who have faced darkness to recognize that within them lies the power to redefine their legacy. It is a journey from victimhood to victory, a narrative of overcoming that serves as a glimmer of hope for others. Through sharing these painful truths, we find strength, not in isolation, but in the collective healing that comes from vulnerability and connection. Together, we can transform our legacies into sources of empowerment, compassion, and boundless love. In the tender years of childhood, our minds are like sponges, absorbing and shaping the essence of our being in ways that linger far beyond those initial moments. During this critical period, I was unwittingly cast into a whirlwind of experiences that no child should ever endure.

These formative years, where the brain is most receptive, laid the groundwork for patterns that would unknowingly draw me into cycles of pain and abuse. It was as if the trauma of my past became a silent architect of my future, designing a path I would spend years trying to redirect.

High school brought its own storms. Reeling from the sting of a first heartbreak, I found myself adrift, craving the warmth of belonging and the solace of being valued. It was during this vulnerable time that I sought comfort in the acceptance of peers, only to find myself in a situation that would leave deep scars on my soul. The aftermath of that night, waking up alone and confused in a dark closet after being raped by several upper-class men, plunged me into a darkness so profound that I believed the only escape was to end my own suffering. My cry for help, and attempt to take my own life, however, was met with laughter, dismissal, and ridicule, intensifying my isolation and despair.

Yet, it was from this abyss of hopelessness that the seeds of resilience began to sprout. At 17, armed with a resolve forged from adversity, I embarked on a journey to redefine my destiny.

Moving across the country, I sought to construct a life defined not by the shadows of my past but by the light of my potential. This leap into the unknown was the first step toward reclaiming my sense of self and purpose.

"We know through painful experience that freedom is never voluntarily given by the oppressor; it must be demanded by the oppressed." - **Martin Luther King**

Years later, as the youngest store manager in a renowned women's apparel chain, I discovered a newfound confidence and stability. It was in this environment, surrounded by wisdom and strength, that I began to envision a future filled with love and security. Falling deeply in love and starting a family seemed to be the culmination of this dream, a chance to break the cycle of abuse that had shadowed my life. However, the promise of happiness was soon clouded by familiar patterns of secrecy and betrayal. The man I had trusted with my heart began to drift away, ensnared by desires that threatened to unravel the life we had built together.

In the wake of this betrayal, I found myself at a crossroads, confronting the painful realization that the love and unity I had so ardently sought were slipping through my fingers. The ultimate act of betrayal by my partner, involving one of my closest friends who had been such a big part of my life, including being there for the birth of our two sons and even signing our marriage certificate, shattered any remnants of trust and safety I had clung. Breaking my heart and starving the nourishment of the friendship I had depended on for fortitude. Yet, even in the face of such profound pain, I remained, anchored by the hope that our family could be mended.

The journey through these trials and many more that continued to escalate over the next five years, though fraught with heartache, have been a profound lesson in the power of resilience, self-love, and the courage to embrace change. It taught me that our legacies are not predetermined by the circumstances of our birth or the trials we endure- but are crafted by the choices we make in the face of those challenges.

In sharing the depths of my journey, my hope is to light a path for those still navigating the shadows of their past, to offer a beacon of hope and a testament to the transformative power of healing and self-discovery. The essence of my story, and indeed the core of my legacy, is not just in overcoming but in the profound understanding and acceptance that our past does not define us; rather, it shapes us into the resilient, compassionate beings we are capable of becoming.

The journey through darkness to find light is a universal one, where the pains and trials of our past serve as the crucible for our growth and evolution. This process of transformation, of moving from victimhood to victory, is not a path walked alone but a shared human experience that connects us all. It is through the acknowledgment of our vulnerabilities and the embracing of our inner strength that we find our true purpose and the ability to inspire change in ourselves and others.

The lessons learned from my past have become the foundation upon which I build my future—not as an unchangeable fate but as a wellspring of motivation and insight. The realization that we are the architects of our reality, that we hold the power to rewrite our narrative and redefine our legacy, is both liberating and empowering. This understanding has not only fueled my passion but has also ignited a mission to empower others to unlock their potential and embrace their true essence through the profound power of the subconscious mind.

As I stand today, reflecting on the journey that has led me to this moment, I am filled with gratitude for every challenge and every obstacle, for they have molded me into the person I am. The unveiling of my book, CRYSTAL CLEAR MINDSET; amidst the towering skyscrapers of the iconic New York Times Square symbolized not just a personal achievement but a message of hope and resilience to all who seek to find their way out of the darkness. It is a reminder that within each of us lies the ability to shine brightly, to overcome adversity, and to live a life of purpose and joy. The blessing of being able to support my local community to empowering global titans of industry like Microsoft is a purpose driven opportunity to spark the real collective transformation my heart has been seeking.

To those who have felt the weight of their past holding them back, know that you are not alone. Your experiences, no matter how difficult, have the power to shape you into a radiant ray of hope and a force for good. The first step towards a brighter future is within your grasp, just one mindset shifts away. Embrace your journey, trust in your strength, and allow your light to shine.

Together, we can rise from the ashes of our past, birthing a new era of healing, love, and legacy that will inspire generations to come.

Repeat after me:

I am worthy of creating my unique legacy.

I am deserving of living my purpose daily.

I am safe to take bold steps in the direction of my heart.

I am able to create the legacy of my choosing.

This story, my legacy, is a testament to the unyielding spirit of the human heart and the boundless capacity for renewal and rebirth. It is my deepest hope that in sharing my journey, you too will find the courage to face your past, to heal, and to step into the magnificent destiny that awaits you. You are a masterpiece in the making, a legacy of hope, and a healing source of light in a world that yearns for your unique brilliance. Remember, the darkest nights produce the brightest stars, and your life is a canvas awaiting the stroke of your greatness.

This narrative, a tapestry woven from threads of pain and resilience, aims to serve as a lighthouse for souls adrift in the tempest of past traumas. Its a declaration that your legacy, despite being shadowed by trials, can be a beacon of hope, a testament to the indomitable spirit within you that yearns for healing and fulfillment.

The essence of this legacy of hope lies not in the erasure of past wounds but in the transformation of these scars into symbols of strength and wisdom. It is a journey that teaches us the power of forgiveness—not just towards others but, most importantly, towards ourselves.

This journey uncovers the truth that our most profound growth often sprouts from the soil of our deepest pain. In embracing our vulnerabilities, we find the courage to forge new paths, to build bridges where walls once stood. This legacy is not about the absence of fear but about the mastery of it, transforming fear from a barrier into a stepping stone towards greater heights. Its about recognizing that the most significant legacy we can leave is one love, compassion, and the unwavering belief in the possibility of renewal.

By sharing this journey, the intention is to weave a collective tapestry of healing, where each thread represents a story of overcoming. Its an invitation to you, the reader, to see your reflections in these words and recognize that you, too, are capable of rewriting the narrative of your life. Its a call to action to embrace your power, to step into the arena of your life with boldness and the conviction that you are the creator of your destiny.

The path towards healing and creating a new legacy is paved with moments of profound insight and transformation. These moments, when we choose love over fear, hope over despair, and light over darkness, are the milestones of our journey. They remind us that every step forward is a step towards becoming the most authentic version of ourselves.

As you embark on this journey of self-discovery and legacy creation, remember that you are not alone. There is a community of fellow travelers, each with their own stories of resilience and hope, walking alongside you. Together, we are building a world where the legacy of hope is not just an individual aspiration but a collective reality.

Your legacy is a masterpiece in progress, a work of art that is uniquely yours. It is shaped by every decision, every challenge, and every triumph. As you continue to navigate the journey of your life, let the legacy of hope be your guiding light, illuminating the path towards a future where your dreams and aspirations are realized.

Let this story be a catalyst for change, a spark that ignites a fire within you to pursue a life of purpose, passion, and profound fulfillment. Stand tall and proud, for you are the architect of a legacy that will inspire, uplift, and empower not only yourself but generations to come.
You are a glimmer of hope in a world eager for your light. Shine brightly, for your legacy is a testament to the limitless potential that resides within each of us to create, to heal, and to love.

In the end, the legacy of hope is more than a story—its a movement, a call to arms for all who have been touched by adversity to rise, to reclaim their power, and to step boldly into the arena of their lives. Its a reminder that the most profound legacies are those born from the heart, fueled by courage, and manifested through the unwavering belief in the transformative power of love and the human spirit.

Who doesn't love a great come back story?

So, as you forge ahead, crafting the legacy you wish to leave behind, remember you are the author of your story, the sculptor of your destiny, and the creator of a legacy that will echo through the ages—a legacy of hope, resilience, and boundless love.

~ CRYSTAL L. PRIVETT ~

Crystal Lynn Privett, Founder of Mindset Service and author of & CRYSTAL-CLEAR MINDSET: among six Bestsellers, is a ray of resilience & empowerment in personal development. Her journey mirrors the transformative power of overcoming adversity. A revered energy psychologist and mental health advocate, she has dedicated her life to unlocking human potential. Her literary works, celebrated for their philanthropic impact, alongside her recognition as a 2x San Diego Power Woman & Women's Leadership Award from the United Nations, underscore her commitment to societal upliftment empowerment.

Nominated as Innovator of the Year by the Carlsbad Chamber of Commerce & Role Model of the Year exemplifies her impact. Sponsoring weekly classes for mental wellness, accessible to all. With a holistic approach blending neuroscience, humor, & empathy, she redefines personal legacies champions sustainable business practices globally. Crystal is an inspirational force, guiding individuals businesses towards success, joy, and impactful legacies.

Contact her for your transformative journey **MindsetService.com.**

1-858-335-7677

~Chapter 9~

Jose Escobar

Leadership, Excellence, and Legacy

Success is a planned event. At least that's what I have come to realize on my journey as an entrepreneur thus far. Nothing happens overnight, and it all takes time, especially when it comes to leaving a legacy. What is legacy? The dictionary will tell you as one of its definitions is the "long lasting impact of particular events and actions that took place in the past, or of a person's life." The thought of creating a legacy for my family has always been top of mind since I was young. The truth of the matter is that creating a legacy is one hundred percent up to me. I find that too many people in the world are waiting for success to come to them, for someone to come save them, and for the resources to fall into their lap.

The reality is that success and legacy always comes down to the work we do at the end of our own arm. My name is Jose Escobar, and I'm the founder and CEO of the Connected Leaders Academy. We are a global community of some of the highest-level entrepreneurs in over forty-five states across the U.S. and nineteen international countries. I know a thing or two about creating impact and legacy. My goal is for you to be inspired and moved to think bigger, create more, and become your best in the pursuit of your own legacy.

Early on at the age of seventeen, I joined network marketing with a company called Amway. I learned so much about the importance of having a positive mental attitude, the importance of personal development, and the power of being in business for yourself. I had many successful entrepreneurs cross my path that would eventually become mentors and coaches in my life. As time went on, I developed myself professionally working for companies like Capital One, PNC Bank, Premier Financial Alliance, Liberty Mutual, and State Farm, while simultaneously evolving as an entrepreneur with various side hustles. Eventually I worked for a global martial arts company under the direct mentorship of the CEO, John Cokinos. I heard golden nugget after golden nugget through the years of working there that would continue to chisel me into a better professional. Given the fact that I always had a "white belt" mentality no matter how good I got, I would inevitably get promoted to Sales Director of the Educational Funding Company (EFC).

I always knew working in the corporate arena that I was an entrepreneur at heart and was not built for a nine to five, forty hours a week for forty years lifestyle. I always felt in the depths of my heart that there was more, that life had more abundance waiting for me, and that this couldn't be all there was in terms of impact, influence, and accomplishment. I had a conviction that I had more to give, more to do, and a legacy to fulfill. No matter how much I tried to apply myself in my professional career, I knew that what I was seeking wouldn't be found in the traditional workspace. I had to spread my wings and explore what the entrepreneurial world had to offer on a higher level.

Upon the realization that being a full-time entrepreneur was my desired path, it ultimately led to a heart-to-heart conversation with my wife on January 15, 2022. She sat me down and expressed to me that she appreciated all the efforts I was making to move our family forward with all the personal development and investments in myself, however, she then hit me with a heart wrenching statement: "at some point you need to start making money in your business." While this was without a doubt a hard pill to swallow, she was right. I had spent well over six figures on courses, programs, books, events, mentors, coaches, etc. and had not yet figured out how to turn that into revenue. (If you are reading this as an entrepreneur, I'm sure you know what I mean.)

As much as that conversation stung, it was exactly what I needed to hear and the catalyst to the exponential growth that my business would soon undergo. That very same day, I took a walk in the neighborhood in my thoughts while smoking a cigar, returned home, locked myself in my office, took some time in prayer and journaling, followed by mind mapping on my white board. This led to the formal launch of my two companies: The Entrepreneur's Bookshelf and the Connected Leaders Academy. I made a commitment to myself and my family that I would show up on a whole new level, embrace every challenge that would come my way, outwork everyone, and make no excuses as I would climb the ladder of success in business.

Upon launching my two new businesses, they quickly began to grow exponentially. In fact, in the first fifteen months, the businesses generated over seven figures organically. (By organically, I mean no website, no paid ads, no funnels or automation, no high-level tech or AI, no CRM, no email lists, or email marketing campaigns.) This was all as simple as word of mouth and strategic use of non-paid social media strategies. With the rapid growth also came new challenges. I've had to overcome the idea that I can do it all and had to start hiring people and building a team. That was an uphill battle regarding selecting the right people and putting the appropriate systems in place. Another unforeseen challenge was making too many financial commitments at one time which of course led to some growing pains. I also had a large global summit event that had to be postponed which came with its own can of worms to overcome. I had to develop high levels of discipline, mental toughness, extreme ownership, commitment, and rhino skin. I feel most people would have caved and thrown in the towel with the amount of pressure, stress, and responsibility that I had to deal with.

Many people just look at the "seven figures in fifteen months organically" piece and think that it was smooth sailing and perhaps luck and right timing. But I can unequivocally say that there were many sleepless nights, tireless days, and tremendous hard work behind the scenes. People don't see the many years of struggle that I had to endure and press through that ultimately led to my success.

As one of my favorite authors, Robin Sharma, has said, *"all change is hard at first, messy in the middle, and gorgeous in the end."* It's been said that every setback is a set up for a comeback. Amid challenges in business, I've developed the ability to be tenacious, to have the grit, perseverance, and determination necessary to push through any speed bump along the way.

Success in anything is uphill all the way, and it is imperative that one accepts this sooner than later because life has its way of bringing challenges that are sometimes self-imposed, but a lot of the time unforeseen. It's impossible to achieve a legacy without hardship, pain, stress, discomfort, and challenges. It's just part of the deal. Embrace it and trust that the tough times don't last. How badly do you want it?

As I overcame challenges and continue to overcome challenges, I realized that what I do ultimately goes back to serving others. I'm inspired when I see members of my community (Connected Leaders Academy) striving for excellence, pursuing the 2.0 version of themselves, and connecting with growth minded entrepreneurs. The purpose behind why I started what I started in business is because I realized so many entrepreneurs are growing their businesses in the same ways. They are plugging into rotary clubs, BNIs, Chambers of Commerce, and local networking events. They are harpooning people on LinkedIn, spear chucking people on Facebook, throwing big nets to see what they can catch in Facebook groups, and throwing darts in DMs to see what sticks.

These strategies lead to virtual meetings where you realize very quickly that you are mutually trying to sell each other. Ultimately nobody sells each other, you end up not being friends anyway, and you wasted an hour of your life that you can never get back.

This leads to burnout, exhaustion, lack of joy in the process of building your business, and frankly, a stagnant business that never scales. This made me realize there had to be a better way (like they say on Shark Tank)! This is precisely why the Connected Leaders Academy was created. I knew that I wanted to invent a brilliant way that entrepreneurs could learn, grow, and connect while scaling their businesses in a way like never before. In the two years that the CLA has been thriving, it brings great joy to my heart to see so many business leaders growing and becoming profitable like never before.

I am all about creating impact, and not just any impact, global impact! I get testimonial after testimonial all the time from members of my community sharing how much they've achieved since joining the tribe. Zig Ziglar said it best: "you can have everything in life you want if you will just help enough other people get what they want." Better and truer words have never been spoken. That's what I do. I serve, I help, I empower, and I lead other leaders to leadership. This is the path I have chosen to create my legacy.

As I reflect on the last two years after launching my business, I can easily say that the process has not been easy, but it has been gratifying. A great mentor of mine once told me, "Jose, we're not here to take up the easy." Life and business are supposed to be hard. It's in overcoming and the pressing through the challenges that we find a sense of achievement and fulfillment.

Sometimes when difficulties come, you must be resourceful. This means you may have to go around, over, under, and sometimes just plow right through the problem. There is no room for excuses. There is no time to waste. Certainly, as they say, idleness is the devil's playground.

Get busy. Get going. And take massive action. (But remember, there is a difference between busy and productive. Productivity yields results. Busyness just means you have no time.) Create the time in your days for your top priorities. Are you creating time for the Lord? Are you creating time for your family? Are you creating time for your health? While scaling and growing your business is important, it ultimately won't matter if the preceding things are not in order. Remember, all of life's domains are interconnected. If your marriage is falling apart, it's hard to be a good parent. If you're not a good parent, it's hard to be a good spouse. If your health is not in order, it becomes seemingly difficult to run your business effectively. If your business isn't run effectively, your finances are out of order. If your finances are out of order, that directly impacts your marriage. Do you see where I am going with this?

To create a legacy, you must be your best across the board. This will require a high level of discipline, consistency, and commitment.

Dolly Parton said, *"if your actions create a legacy that inspires others to dream more, learn more, do more, and become more, then, you are an excellent leader."*

This is what I aspire towards. If I had to sum up what I love to do, this quote hits the nail on the head. Legacy begins in the home. How am I showing up for my significant other? My kids? I cannot be a true leader in the business world if my household is falling apart. Part of this journey requires me to show up EVERY SINGLE DAY. Is it hard? You bet. Do I fall short sometimes? Absolutely. The point is that I expect a lot of myself, but one of the things I don't expect is perfection. Although, I do strive for excellence. I say all the time that I want my kids to catch me as often as possible in the act of excellence.

Aristotle once said, *"we are what we repeatedly do; excellence, then, is not an act, but a habit."* I strive to pass this baton of excellence to my children. I know I can be better, but the difference between me and most is that I am in the pursuit of excellence all the time. I want it. How bad do you want it?

We are all leaders in this life, whether you have a business or not. Some of you lead in your job, some of you lead in your home, or perhaps in the recreational space. You might lead in your church or in your social circles, but leadership begins with yourself. You must be able to lead yourself to the highest level. Only when you hold yourself to a high standard and lead yourself first can you, in turn, lead others effectively. In my opinion, there is a direct correlation between the level of leadership you have and the heights of legacy you leave behind.

My encouragement to you today is to think about what legacy you want to leave behind. What will future generations say about you when you are gone? The fact that I am writing this chapter in this book is part of my legacy creation. Do you know why? Books live on for centuries and beyond. Have you noticed that people don't throw away books, they donate them? It's time. TODAY! NOW! Start creating a plan to outlive your life. Will you be spoken of in a positive light decades and centuries after your death? Are people better off because you lived?

Everything I do in life and business today is in direct alignment with the legacy I plan to leave behind. Put the pen to the paper and decide what yours will look like. They say you only live once, I say, you only die once, and you live daily. Be your best, live fully alive, create your own legacy. Your family deserves it. You deserve it! Now get after it!

~Jose Escobar ~

Jose Escobar, an acclaimed personal development speaker and 10x published author, leads two successful businesses: The Entrepreneur's Bookshelf and the Connected Leaders Academy that has surpassed over 7-figures in fifteen months organically. He engages with entrepreneurs and advanced leaders, collectively reaching over thirty million through presentations and coaching programs. He works with over 350 successful leaders globally. Jose is a master sales professional. He is happily married with five kids. Discover more about Jose's offerings at:

www.ConnectedLeadersAcademy.com

"You can't buy a legacy, YOU BUILD IT! "

~ Lori A. McNeil

~ Lori A. McNeil ~

Creator & Founder of Legacy Builders, Legacy Impact Podcast, Legacy Unlimited Magazine & Author of Legacy Unlocked

Lori is an International Media, Marketing, and Branding Expert who specializes in helping entrepreneurs and business leaders understand the power of developing one cohesive plan. She is a powerful speaker who empowers and inspires others to step into their greatness and use Media to reach more people and increase sales.

Lori was selected as an official speaker for the Think & Grow Rich World Legacy Tour and was invited as a Featured Speaker for Turning Point 20/20 with 2.25 million people attending live. She is featured in media over five hundred times a year and her global work earned her the Lifetime Presidential Service Award 2x under two different Presidential Administrations; most recently, the Global Visionary Leader Award, as well as special leadership recognition as a Global Legacy Builder by the L.A. Tribune and the prestigious Trailblazer award by the NOW foundation.

www.lorimcneil.com

www.ingramcontent.com/pod-product-compliance
Lightning Source LLC
Chambersburg PA
CBHW071409220526
45469CB00004B/1220